NAMIB

Author's other books

Mountain Odyssey in Southern Africa,
with James Clarke

Different Drums: Reflections on a Changing Africa,
with Michael Wood

The Lost World of the Kalahari
(thirtieth-anniversary illustrated edition),
with Laurens van der Post

First published in Great Britain in 1991
by Sidgwick & Jackson Limited

Maps by Francesca Pelizzoli

ISBN 0-283-99960-8

Photoset by Rowland Phototypesetting Limited
Bury St Edmunds, Suffolk
Printed by Eagle Colourbooks Limited, Blantyre, Glasgow
Bound by The Bath Press Limited, Bath
for Sidgwick & Jackson Limited
Cavaye Place
London SW10 9PG

PREVIOUS PAGES: *Goliath heron on the Cunene River*

THIS PAGE: *Gemsbok in the northern dune sea near the Hartmann valley*

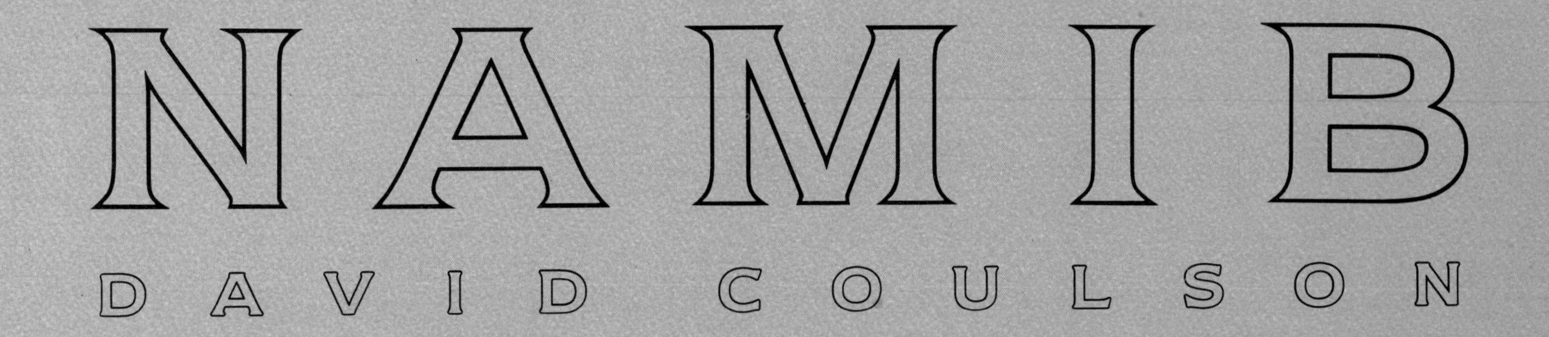

DESIGN BY BARNEY WAN

SIDGWICK & JACKSON
LONDON

PREFACE

Snow was falling silently outside the window as I lay on my bed immersed in a book in a centrally-heated house in Sweden. I was twelve years old and the book was *A Twist of Sand* by Geoffrey Jenkins, a war thriller set in the Namib desert of South West Africa. Twenty-nine years later the fascination which originally stemmed from reading that paperback has led to the publication of my own book on the Namib.

My first visit to Namibia (formerly South West Africa) was in 1973. I went as a tourist, with a camera and a girlfriend. I was already a keen amateur photographer, and several of my photographs from that safari are reproduced in this book. Hooked by the great open spaces, wild mountain ranges and huge dunes of sand, I returned in 1976, exploring new areas and taking more photographs. During a two-week period I covered six thousand miles of dirt roads in my blue Chevrolet saloon. I had already travelled widely in Africa, but Namibia and its coastal desert made a dramatic and lasting impact on me. Here were areas where one had the strong sensation of being the first human intruder.

Following a 1979 exhibition of my photographs in London, I was commissioned by Macmillan to take the pictures for a book on the wild mountain regions of Southern Africa, including Namibia. This was a turning point in my life. I abandoned my career in management consultancy and took off into the mountains on a thirty-thousand-mile solo journey. I spent two months in Namibia gathering material, and in 1981 joined the Kaokoland Desert Elephant Expedition led by Clive Walker, then chairman of the Endangered Wildlife Trust of Southern Africa. In the Hoanib Valley, on the mountainous border of Kaokoland and Damaraland, I took my first photographs of the desert elephants of the Namib. The book which resulted from this journey, *Mountain Odyssey*, appeared in 1984, with text by journalist James Clarke incorporating extracts from my diary.

Four years later I returned, this time taking photographs of the Namib for an article in the *Smithsonian* magazine. On this trip I enjoyed my first glimpses of the forbidding Skeleton Coast, so vividly described in *A Twist of Sand*. The following year I produced a photo essay on the wild horses of the Namib, with Brian Jackman, for the *Sunday Times Magazine*, and a similar article for *Optima*. These trips provided me with pictures of a dramatic and romantic story. When the article was published in the *Sunday Times* I was in Botswana photographing for the *Lost World of the Kalahari*, a joint project with Laurens van der Post marking the thirtieth anniversary of his classic desert journey. It was therefore some time before I saw the *Sunday Times* piece but Carey Smith, then commissioning editor for Sidgwick & Jackson, spotted it in London and eventually tracked me down in the Kalahari desert. It was she who started the process which led to this book being published.

Fortunately I already had many of the photographs I needed, but there were gaps, and to fill these I returned to Namibia in late 1988. The trip was dogged by breakdowns, but was nevertheless productive, and in March the following year I returned for a final eight-thousand-mile safari, during which I took the remaining photographs.

I am extremely fortunate to have travelled to Namibia's remotest areas. Apart from the sheer size of the country and the inaccessibility of many of its regions, large tracts of it are closed to the public. These include the diamond mining and conservation areas and the military zones, most of which happen to fall within the Namib. The authorities took the view that the favourable publicity resulting from my work would be to their benefit, and gave me their support, without which I could not have undertaken this project.

I have based my text on the diaries I kept on my trips. In the process I have endeavoured to give an impression of the Namib's diversity and beauty. I am not a scientist and do not pretend to be an expert on the subjects discussed. The library and museum in Windhoek are recommended for those interested in further reading.

My hope is that this book will serve as an introduction to a part of the world that few people have seen and through which I have been privileged to travel. My aim has been to share these experiences and the information I have gleaned from friends, many of whom are indeed experts.

When referring to ethnic groups I have not always adhered to the nomenclature preferred by anthropologists. The term 'Bushman' is sometimes considered derogatory these days. He is either a 'hunter gatherer' or 'San'. The name 'Hottentot' is also deemed by some to be belittling. He should be 'Khoi'. Because I am not an anthropologist and many of my readers may not be familiar with the terms 'San' and 'Khoi', I have often used their more familiar names. In so doing I mean no offence to the 'Khoisan' people. The same goes for any references to 'Bergdamara' and 'Strandlopers', names also now considered by some to be pejorative and not definitive.

In writing about the Skeleton Coast I am referring to the whole Namib coastline, not just the northern stretch of coast that falls within the Skeleton Coast National Park. The name pre-dates the park and applies to a bigger region. I also refer on occasions to the 'diamond coast', by which I mean the coastline between Walvis Bay and Alexander Bay, where most of the diamonds have been recovered over the years.

Because Namibia has been inhabited by many tribes, and has fallen under the influence of different countries with different languages, there are often alternative spellings for place names. I have therefore chosen the ones with which I am familiar and tried to be consistent throughout the text.

Photography in the Namib is not just a question of equipment and technique. In the desert, for example, the light is so dazzling that colours are washed out and flat for all but the first and the last two hours of each day. Travelling has to be precisely planned and I have often found myself driving hundreds of miles in order to photograph a particular spot in the right light. Sometimes I have been thwarted by misty or hazy conditions, but at other times the sky will fill with wonderful cumulus rain clouds adding beauty and drama to the scene. There are also plants that only flower at times dictated by certain weather conditions and animals that only appear in certain places at certain times. It is only through the continued support and advice of friends and through years of experimentation and learning that I have been able to attempt to do justice to the subject.

For camera equipment I carry Nikon (35mm) F3s and a small range of interchangeable lenses ranging from my 28mm wide-angle lens to a 400mm telephoto. I use Fujichrome and Kodachrome film, protected from the heat in cool boxes. During the cold desert nights, I open the boxes, closing them again at sunrise. Sand and dust are a constant menance, but sealable bags keep them at bay. Every night after sunset I clean my equipment with a paint brush and cloth, and sometimes a dust gun. The only filter I have used for these photographs is a polarizing one.

This book has been a labour of love, a tribute to a part of the world that has enriched my life. If only a fraction of the pleasure and stimulus I have experienced is transmitted in these pages the project will have been worthwhile.

David Coulson
Karen, Nairobi 1990

CONTENTS

OPPOSITE: Dawn on the Cunene estuary

ACKNOWLEDGEMENTS

In 1988 I was driving along a lonely road in northern Namibia about a hundred miles from the nearest town, when my newly-overhauled engine seized. After a nine-hour wait, a vehicle passed – an army doctor driving south from the Angola border. He knew who I was, having seen me at a bar with a mutual friend, Chris Eyre, the week before, and knew about my work. He could do nothing to help me but promised to radio Chris from the next police post. As his dust trail receded over the horizon I brewed more tea in the shade of my Land-cruiser, and five hours later Chris arrived with a tow bar, a cold beer and Jason, his fox terrier. He took me back to his house in Opuwa, and four days later two mechanics drove 500 miles from Windhoek with a replacement engine, which they installed free of charge.

I tell this story to illustrate how reliant one is, in a country like Namibia, on one's friends who live there. The AA (Automobile Association) does not provide a rescue service in the desert, and if something goes wrong you are on your own. Without the help of such friends my task would have been all but impossible.

Namibia's national parks and conservation areas are administered by the Directorate of Nature Conservation, which falls under the Department of Agriculture and Fisheries. The department has always been helpful in organizing the necessary permissions and logistical back-up for my trips. I would particularly like to thank the following who have so often assisted me: Dr Schneider, Polla Swart, Jan Joubert, Robbie Hawthorne, Rudi Loutit, Tony Williams, Hu Berry, Rod Braby, Peter Tarr, Duncan Gilchrist, Derek and Jenny Clark and many others who have assisted at different times.

The other authority which has given me exceptional support and access is CDM (Consolidated Diamond Mines of South West Africa). As a result I have been able to visit areas never photographed before. I am especially grateful to the following at Oranjemund and Luderitz: Keith Whitelock, Roger Burchell, Bert de Jager, Jan Coetzer, Wynand Breytenbach and Ken Williams. In Windhoek Clive Cowley helped me on many occasions over several years.

After so many trips Namibia has become like a second home for me. A number of my friends are mentioned in the text, but a few are not. Of these I should like especially to thank Pieter Mostert and Amy Schoeman. I first met Pieter in the Richtersveld in 1981 with Piet van der Westhuizen when I was photographing for *Mountain Odyssey*. Ever since then he has been a loyal and welcoming friend with whom I have based myself on many occasions. I met Amy Schoeman in 1981 when she was still with the Department of Nature Conservation. Much of my initial inspiration and advice came from Amy, who knows the Namib so well.

In the field, Chris Eyre and Garth Owen-Smith have been my particular friends and 'gurus'. They are both exceptional people with whom I have shared special times. Other friends who have gone out of their way to help, or with whom I have travelled, include: Piet van der Westhuizen, Blythe Loutit, Mary Seely, Rod and Sigi Braby, Gino and Kathy Noli, John Patterson, Paul and Marlene Coulson, Sharon Montgomery, Eckhardt and Kathy Klenkler and Suzanne Nicholson.

All the colour photographs in this book were taken by me, with the exception of four which I am proud to include. The photograph of the three desert elephants crossing the dunes on page 75 was taken by Gavin Thompson (Windhoek). The lion feeding on the carcass of a whale (pages 114–15) was photographed by the conservator John Patterson. The photographs of a gecko (page 52) and a brown hyena (page 99) were taken by Peter Tarr of Nature Conservation. I am very grateful to them.

Most of the old black and white photographs are reproduced by courtesy of the Windhoek State Archives. Some of the early mining photographs come from CDM's archives and some of the photographs of the *Dunedin Star* from the South African Naval Archives.

When travelling in the desert one is totally dependent on one's vehicle. Having already served me well in the Kalahari, my Toyota Landcruiser was once again a trusty friend, carrying me 15,000 miles in 1988 and 1989 to every corner of the Namib. I have also travelled extensively in Landcruisers kindly provided by the Directorate of Nature Conservation. I have great respect for them.

Outside Namibia I am indebted to the following friends in South Africa for their enthusiastic help and back-up: Keith and Elizabeth Alexander, Malcolm and Anne Badham, Tom Bedford, John and Veda Carver, Victor Hugo, Martin Louw and the Renton family, who have also provided a temporary home for my Land-cruiser in my absence. In Kenya the Nightingales generously invited me to write my text on their farm above Lake Naivasha while Jill Sowerby typed it in Nairobi. I cannot thank her enough for struggling with my scrawl for so many long hours. I am also extremely grateful to Mike Eldon for editing the first drafts and helping me shape the book. As usual, Pauline Mousley gave me secretarial back-up and Nicky Blundell-Brown lost no opportunity in promoting my interests.

While I was in Africa Mary Claire Gibson looked after my affairs in London, which I greatly appreciated, and on my return Ashley Nicholas and Jan Gillett of the Royal Botanic Gardens, Kew, kindly identified my more obscure plant photographs. I would also like to thank Libby Joy for editing the book so patiently and imaginatively. Fellow photographers and soul mates Angela Fisher and Carol Beckwith spent invaluable hours with me helping to cut down the thousands of photographs to a manageable and representative collection. Carol generously allowed us the use of her flat to design the book. Richard Nightingale and Eva Monley helped in many ways, as always; and my parents gave administrative and moral support. I am most grateful to Laurens van der Post for allowing me to quote the lines that appear on the back of the book.

Of all the contributors to this book the person to whom I owe most, however, is Barney Wan, who designed it. Generous, thoughtful, imaginative, Barney is not only a brilliant designer but is also an outstanding cook, so the long hours in Carol's flat were often interrupted by delicious lunch breaks. I am truly thankful to Barney for all his amazing work.

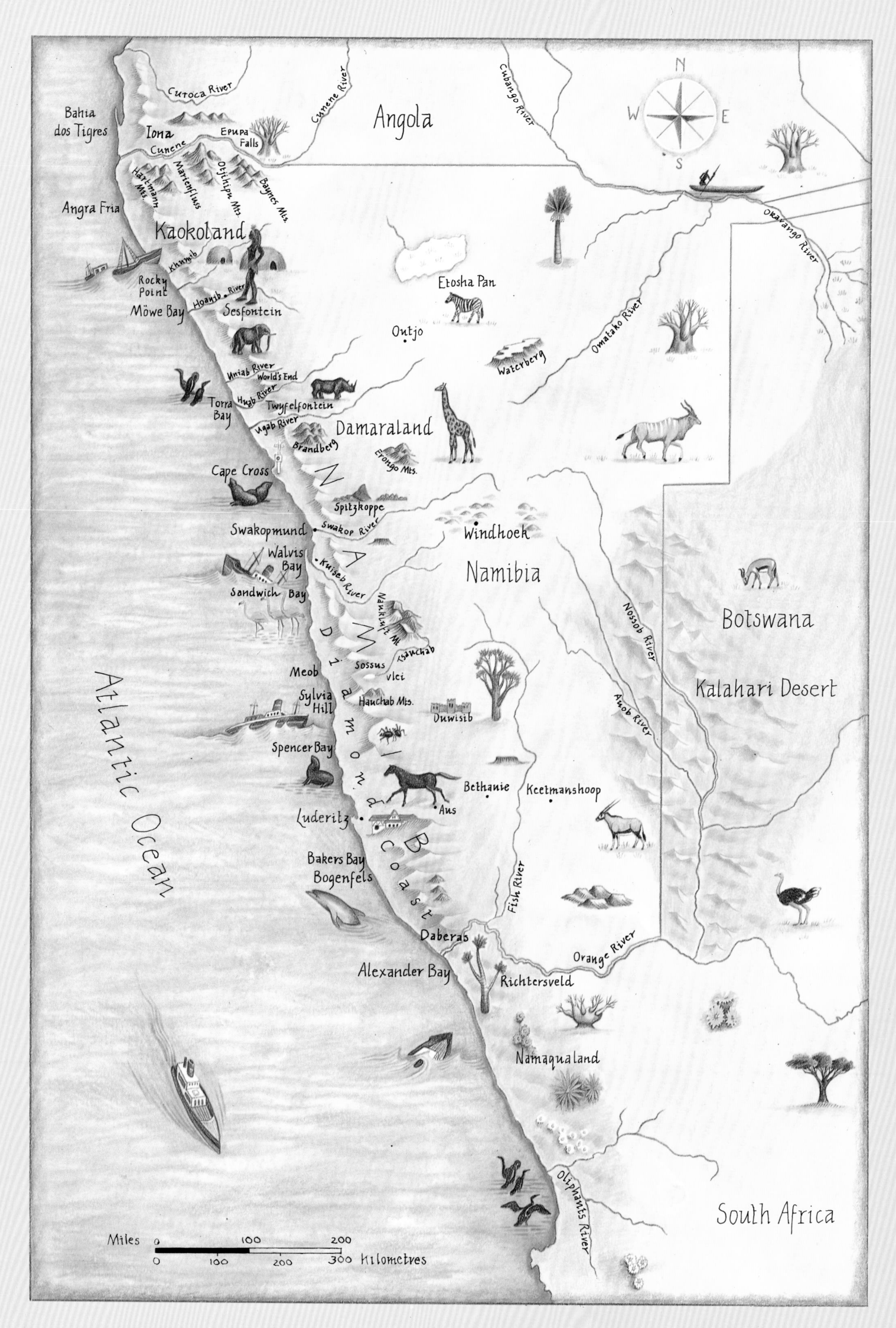

THE NAMIB DESERT

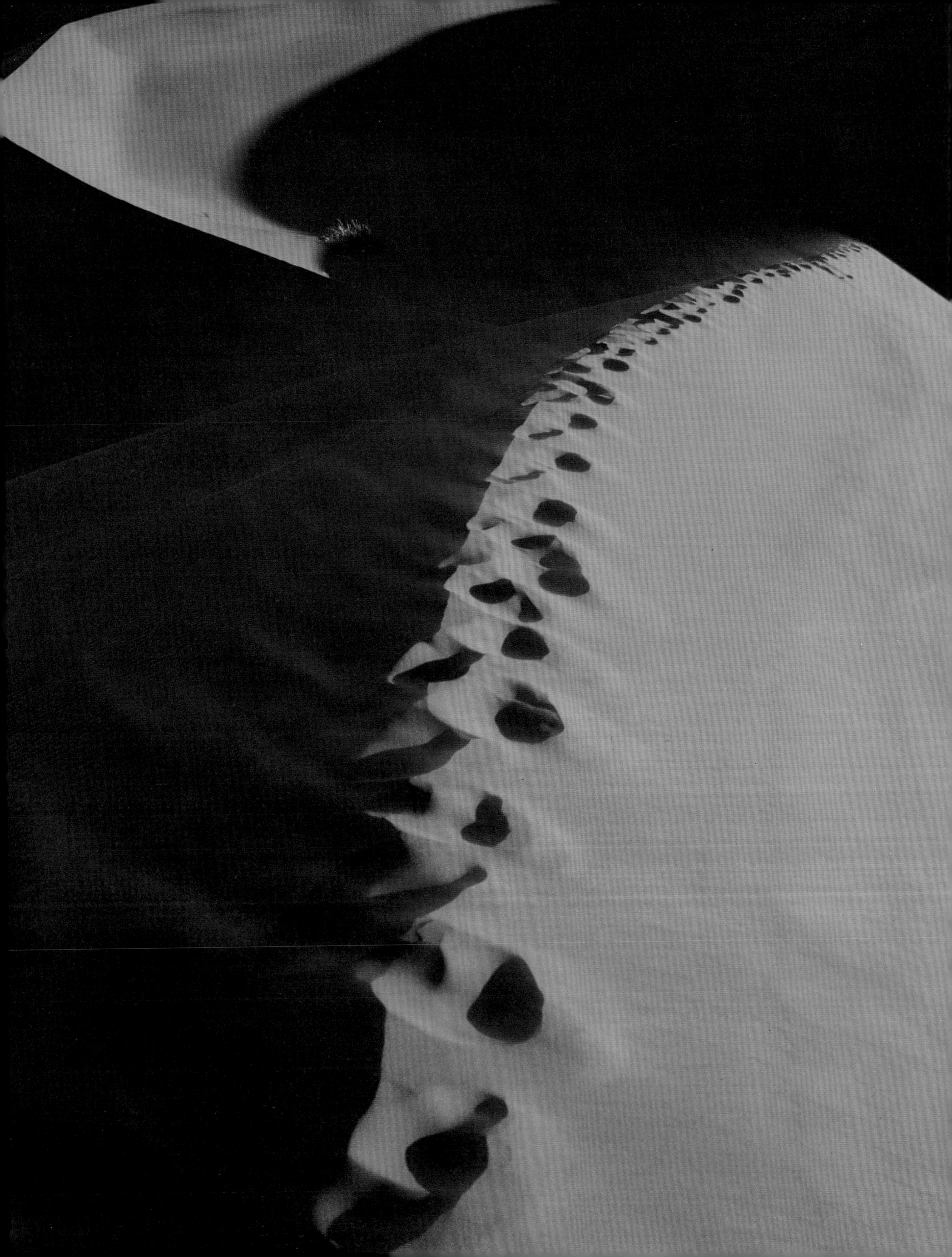

CHAPTER ONE

A Secret World

In a remote corner of south western Africa is a desolate paradise that few outsiders have ever heard of, and fewer still have visited. The Nama and Bushmen people who once inhabited parts of this coastal desert called it 'Namib', meaning endless expanse. To them the desert was no stranger. Unlike the sailors and foreign travellers who feared its terrifying desolation, they were able to survive, knowing the location of secret springs and food sources. The Namib covers an area of over a hundred thousand square miles, most of which is an uninhabited wilderness of sand-dunes, plains and mountains. Man's role in this land has usually been confined to that of visitor. Here the forces of nature reign supreme.

The desert begins in southern Angola and stretches 1,300 miles down the Namibian coast, until it peters out at the Oliphants (Elephants) River in Namaqualand, South Africa. Its desert shore is known as the Skeleton Coast due to the many ships that have been wrecked there over the centuries. Only a hundred miles wide from east to west, it attracts an average annual rainfall of less than half an inch a year. There are places which have had no rain this century.

When I think of the Namib it is the sand that fills my memories and imagination, for this area is the home of some of the world's highest sand-dunes. There are two main dune fields or dune seas. The largest of these blankets a vast tract of country between the Orange River and Walvis Bay, while the smaller one stretches northwards from Torra Bay to the Angola border. Here it is halted by the fast-flowing Cunene River. On the Angolan side the sands regroup and the dune sea re-establishes itself in the area known as the Iona National Park.

The desert can be bleak or beautiful depending on the weather prevailing. In fog or cloud the dunes present a grey, forbidding backdrop, yet in evening sunlight they glow with the intensity of living coals. The sands inland are redder than those at the coast. The Kalahari sands, to the east of the Namib, are the reddest of all – almost tomato red. In the Namib the colour of the sands may change dramatically in the course of a single day. From the deep reds and ambers of the early morning the colours fragment into a subtle patchwork of pastel yellows, browns and mauves. At the same time, the long dark shadows of the early morning and evening gradually condense, disappear and re-emerge in a different afternoon configuration. A dune that appears in a certain shape and form by morning light may be barely recognizable in the afternoon.

I am irresistibly drawn to sand-dunes, intoxicated by their subtle shapes and sensuous curves, aware of the light and shade and the network of strange little animal tracks left from the night before – evidence of the life within. At other times, when the wind blows, the slopes and slipfaces are covered in an ethereal, steam-like layer of wind-blown sand, moaning and roaring through gullies and depressions. On winter nights the fog creeps in spilling into valleys and hollows, carpeting them in soft cotton wool.

These mountains of sand are not inert or static, but dynamic, always moving and changing, depending on the strength and direction of the winds. Some are big, some small, some fast moving, some slow. Some are highly mobile, moving over fifty feet a year swallowing up anything that happens to be in their path. These are called 'barchans', which are crescent-shaped and normally found in areas where sand has encroached on the gravel plains, rather than in the big dune fields.

OPPOSITE: *My footprints in the Namib dunes*

The highest formations in the Namib are the 'star dunes' near Sossusvlei, whose shape has resulted from winds blowing from several different directions. These are the slowest moving dunes, their bases stabilized by tussock grass and other vegetation.

The slipface is where the desert's microlife thrives, the most densely inhabited part of the dune ecosystem. A wide variety of lizards, beetles, spiders, rodents and snakes live here, some unique to the Namib. The beetles and lizards pop in and out of the sands to regulate their temperature and escape from predators. Jackals are the most frequent large predator in the dunes, hyena being less common. The gemsbok (oryx) is at home in the dunes but normally only found in small numbers because of the sparse grazing. Near the border of Kaokoland and Damaraland, in the northern dune sea, you can sometimes see elephant on their way to age-old water-holes. Occasionally they take the quick way down a slipface, on their backsides.

Between the Hoanib and Cunene Rivers is Kaokoland, a vast tract of country over fifty thousand square miles in extent, one of Africa's least known but most beautiful areas. Criss-crossed with rugged mountain ranges and deep valleys, it also boasts plains as vast as East Africa's Serengeti. Prior to the 1970s, much of Kaokoland fell within the old Etosha Pan Game Reserve. In those days the Reserve stretched all the way to the Atlantic coast, making it one of the biggest in the world, but the western area has always been closed to tourism. Since the recent cease-fire, however, Kaokoland has become more accessible and much of the western region has once again been proclaimed a reserve. Until very recently outsiders were not allowed in without special permission from the authorities, which was not normally granted. This was because there were few roads and the region is wild and inaccessible. Coupled with this was the fact that diamonds are known to exist near the coast and the authorities wanted to discourage diamond smuggling. In recent years the north-eastern part of Kaokoland has fallen into the SWAPO (South West Africa People's Organization) war theatre – the 'Operational Zone'. For more than twenty years of war it has been a high-risk area, where freedom fighters were occasionally intercepted, some of whom planted land-mines in the roads. (South West Africa is the old name for Namibia.)

One of the wildest and most spectacular parts of Kaokoland is the mountainous area where the jade-green Cunene winds its lonely way through a desolate valley, often thousands of feet deep, separating Namibia from Angola. Impressive ranges like the Hartmanns, Otjihipus and Baynes mountains dominate the barren landscape; in the west the Hartmanns merge with the dune sea.

Normally this is an austere world of rock and sand but occasionally rain falls. On these rare occasions the valleys are transformed into a paradise, carpeted in dense grass with wild flowers and huge congregations of springbok, gemsbok, ostriches and giraffe. Gradually the grass dries out and dies, turning from lush green to gold, rippled into a thousand different patterns by the wind. Even the secretive mountain zebra zigzag down from rocky passes to join the party on the plain.

These plains and mountains are the home of the Himba people, tall independent nomads who live in isolated communities, tucked away in remote valleys. Like the wildlife of the region, they move as the rain and grazing dictate, leading their cattle and goats to ancestral water-holes. Unlike their Herero cousins, whose flamboyant style of dress was influenced by the wives of early missionaries, they dress traditionally, in skins. The women use ochre make-up like the Maasai in East Africa.

PREVIOUS PAGES: *Early morning on the crest of a dune*

OPPOSITE: *Below the slipface of a seventy-foot barchan dune*

FOLLOWING PAGES: *A Himba nomad looking out over the Namib in Western Kaokoland*

South of the Hoanib valley is Damaraland, a rugged rock-strewn wilderness cut through from east to west by sand rivers. These are a special feature of the Namib, dry watercourses that only rarely flow after exceptional rainfall. Even when they do it is normally for two or three days at most. Under the surface these linear oases may flow for much longer, and underground pools and moisture can persist for more than a year, enabling plants and shrubs to survive. Damaraland's major sand rivers are the Uniab, Huab, and Ugab, whose valleys and tributaries are the last retreat of Namibia's desert elephant and rhino. To see these leviathans crossing the bare lava desert, or negotiating the dunes near the Hoanib delta, is one of the greatest sights the Namib has to offer.

Once, in a different climatic era, the region teemed with game – as evidenced by the mass of animal rock-engravings and paintings found in the mountains. South of the Ugab, Damaraland is dominated by a huge hulk of a mountain, the Brandberg, whose red rock-faces glow like embers at sunset, visible from far around. Its hot, inaccessible valleys are a 'gallery' of ancient rock art and rare flora. The paintings were made by Bushmen, the original inhabitants of Southern Africa, who lived in the Namib for thousands of years. I can clearly see them in my imagination, small bands trotting easily across the plains between mountains, with their bows and quivers of arrows, diminutive figures in a vast landscape. The desert held no fears for them and they left a vivid record of their lives and dreams in the caves and rock shelters of their mountain world. These little men have now vanished. Only traces of their mongolian features were left in the occasional face of a Damara pastoralist. One of Namibia's earliest peoples, the Damara, were once slaves to the Nama (Hottentots), who shared a common origin with the Bushmen. Later they were slaves to the Hereros and remained so until early this century. Their own language has long since disappeared and they now speak a language similar to Nama. The Bergdamara were hunter-gatherers who lived in remote mountain ranges such as the Erongo, the Brandberg, and the giant Spitzkoppe, which rises tooth-like from the euphorbia plains of southern Damaraland. Sometimes called Namibia's Matterhorn, the Spitzkoppe is the gateway to the plains and canyons of the central Namib.

Two important sand rivers traverse these central plains, the Swakop and the Kuiseb. Both have gouged impressive canyons through the desert, whose labyrinthine gorges are known as the gramadullas, meaning 'moonscape' or 'back of beyond'. I can imagine the dismay of early pioneers when they first set eyes on those badlands. For the last eighty miles of its north-westerly journey to the sea, the Kuiseb cuts straight across the desert, forming a dividing line between the southern dune sea and the plains. When the northward-moving dunes reach the Kuiseb they spill into it, the overspill being washed away by the flood when the river comes down after the rains. At such times thousands of tons of sand are carried downstream to the coast. In the lower reaches of the Kuiseb, at the foot of the dunes, live a proud remnant of the Hottentot people, the Topnaars. Historically the Topnaars have always been intimately associated with the Namib, living in the riverbed oases and sometimes even along the Skeleton Coast itself.

Since the early part of the century, vast tracts of the southern Namib have been closed to the outside world. This is because there are diamonds there for the taking, under the sand and in the rocky crevices. Before World War I, in an effort to control the free-for-all which followed the first diamond discoveries, the German Government proclaimed thousands of square miles of desert a 'Sperrgebiet', or forbidden area. (Namibia was a German colony in those days.) Most of this Sperrgebiet is wilderness. The diamonds were only found in a fifteen-mile strip along the coastline,

PREVIOUS PAGES: *Carving its way through a wilderness of rock and sand, the Cunene River is the frontier between Angola and Namibia*

OPPOSITE AND FOLLOWING PAGES: *Rainfall in Kaokoland*

ABOVE: *Skeleton of a chameleon*

OPPOSITE: *A side-winding ('horned') adder negotiating the dunes*

BELOW: *Bird tracks on the sand*

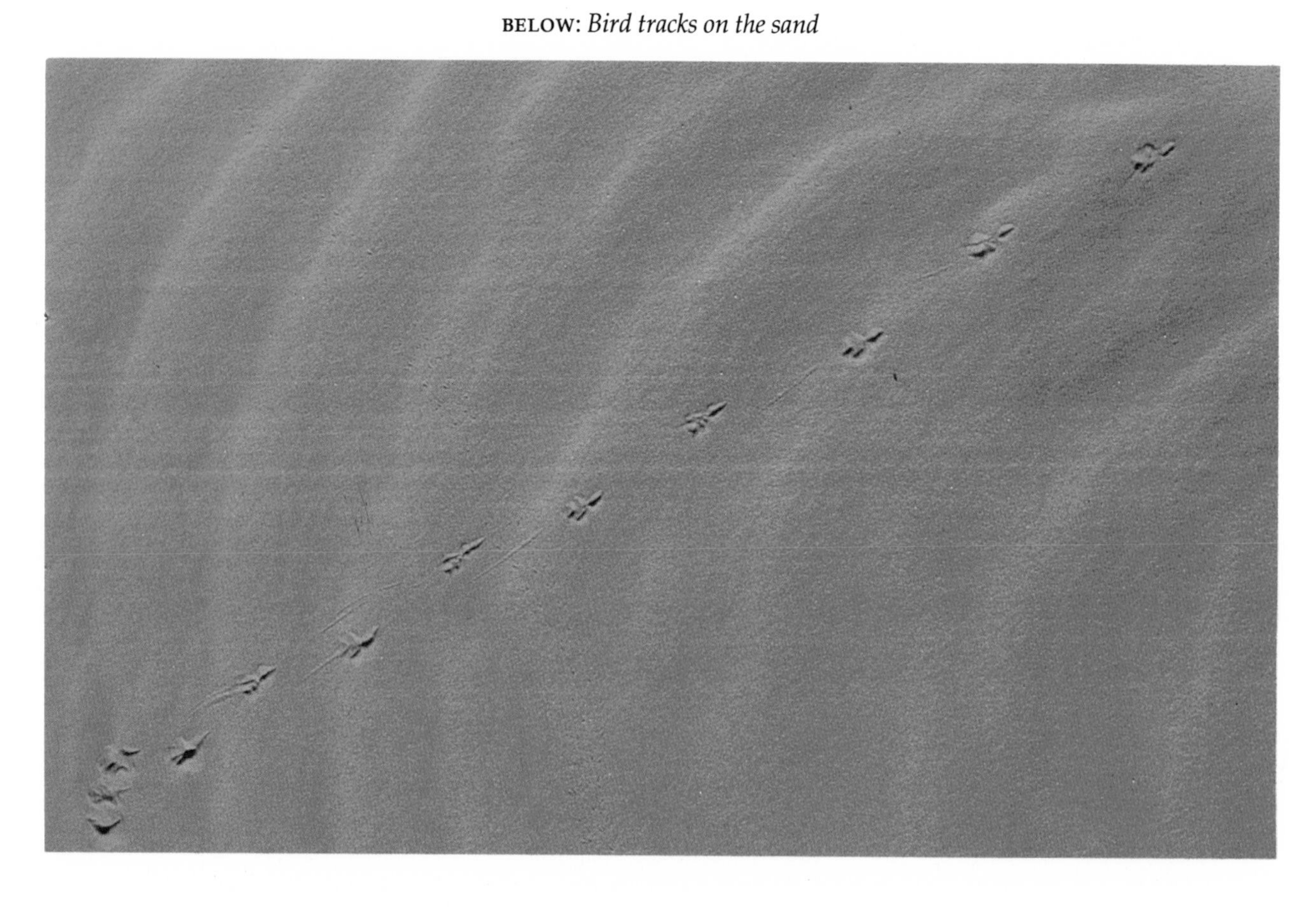

mainly between the Orange River and the port of Luderitz. Today diamond mining is restricted to the terraces near the Orange River mouth. The little German towns that sprang up during the diamond rush were long ago abandoned to the wind and sand – ghost towns in the forbidden area. Inland are sandy plains and island mountains which few Westerners have explored. Once they were inhabited by Bushmen.

The Orange River is perennial, like the Cunene, and forms the international border between Namibia and the Cape Province of South Africa. Immediately south of the river in Namaqualand is an area of rugged mountains known as the Richtersveld, a maze of gorges and knife-edge ridges. Rich in minerals and rare plants, the area has long attracted prospectors and botanists alike. Namaqualand is famous for its springtime flowering, especially on the rolling plains which stretch south towards the Oliphants River. At the height of the season, its sandy flats are transformed into a solid mass of purples, reds and golds.

For me the most spectacular feature of the Namib is its coastline, the notorious Skeleton Coast. Here Africa comes face to face with Antarctica. Giant desert dunes descend to the cold ocean waters, chilled by the Benguela current which flows north, fresh from the Antarctic. At this meeting of extremes both the desert and the sea are at their wildest. Senses are sharpened, moods are stronger and feelings run deeper. The awesome power of the elements is overwhelming, brought vividly home by the skeletons of ships and men lying scattered and crushed on its shores. Blue-green rollers rumble on to untouched beaches where colonies of sea-birds rest in their

PREVIOUS PAGES: *Knowing the location of remote desert springs, the gemsbok (oryx) go for long periods without water or grazing*

BELOW: *A forest of quiver trees, or kokerboom,* (Aloe dichotoma)*, whose wood the Bushmen used for their arrows*

ABOVE: *After rain, the Hartmann's mountain zebra come down to graze*

FOLLOWING PAGES 30–1: *The Great Spitzkoppe (5,669 feet) in Southern Damaraland*

FOLLOWING PAGES 32–3: *Wreck of the* Shaunee, *an American trawler beached near Sandwich Bay in 1976*

thousands between fishing forays. Occasionally the birds make way for foraging jackals, brown hyenas, seals, penguins and even lions.

In the late afternoon an ominous fog gathers out to sea, gradually advancing towards the shore. It rolls inexorably in, blotting out the sun, turning summer into winter, probing into the desert dunes and blanketing them with chilly life-giving moisture. It is the prevailing south-westerly winds which bring the fog, as well as the ice-cold air from the Antarctic. This routine only changes when the east wind blows strongly from the interior, pushing the cold air back out to sea. Suddenly temperatures soar from the fifties and sixties to well over a hundred degrees Fahrenheit. Hurricane-force winds scour the surface of the desert, whipping up sandstorms and blotting out the sun. Eerily they howl and moan through the dunes, until they finally die and the fog creeps back.

CHAPTER TWO

Living Mirage

In the southern part of the Namib, just south of the Orange River in Namaqualand, is an area called the Richtersveld. Known as much for its arid mountain scenery and incredible rock colours as for its unique plant life, it is also rich in minerals, including copper and diamonds. There are no roads here, just very rough tracks that zigzag across the most rugged country imaginable. You plunge down into deep ravines, follow tortuous sand-river gorges, snake up boulder-strewn slopes, negotiate knife-edge ridges and find that as the crow flies you have hardly gone anywhere at all. This is wild country: there are no road signs, and few accurate maps exist. Prospectors surveyed the area a generation ago and many of their vehicle tracks are as fresh as if they were made yesterday. But if you make the mistake of following them, as likely as not they will lead you on a long circuitous route that will terminate in a dead-end. Some of these prospectors clearly had a sense of humour. I remember finding a rusty old sign with an animal skull on top giving the distances to London, New York and Cairo.

I first visited the Richtersveld in 1981 with Piet van der Westhuizen, who was then the Nature Conservator responsible for northern Namaqualand. It was October, the Southern African spring, and clumps of mauve mesembryanthemums ('mesums') and brilliantly coloured Namaqualand daisies grew everywhere. The overall effect was of a beautiful rock garden on a grand scale. Unlike the central and northern Namib, this area receives a sparse winter rainfall giving rise to a springtime blooming of the famous wild flowers of Namaqualand.

Approaching the south we wound our way along a deep ravine and camped at the foot of a mountain called the Rosyntjieberg ('rosyntjie' means raisin, referring to the many cracks and fissures which criss-cross the mauve rock faces). After sunset the mountain turned the colour of burgundy against an already star-studded sky.

In the small hours of the following morning a sharp gale warned us of a change in weather. The stars disappeared and we heard distant thunder reverberating through the mountains. Lightning flashed, illuminating the cliffs around us, and I caught the smell of damp dust before a storm. The thunder got louder and the chances of getting caught by the first real downpour the Richtersveld had seen in years seemed a real possibility. It would be just my luck. At 5.30 large drops of rain began to fall. By the time I had jumped out of my sleeping bag, rapidly gathering my things together, it began to pelt down. Piet was also jumping around, cursing and grabbing his clothes. Prolonged rain in the area would have completely trapped us, the only access to this valley being via the narrow gorge by which we had entered. Heavy rain would rapidly make an exit impossible. Yet fortunately the rain lasted a mere five minutes and we were able to laugh it off.

After an early breakfast we wound our way up a dramatic pass and descended on the coastal side to a hill known as Cornell's Kop. Cornell was an eccentric explorer who travelled to many corners of the southern Namib in the first two decades of this century. He participated in the diamond rush near Luderitz in 1908 and 1909, and came within an ace of discovering the incredibly rich diamond fields near the Orange River mouth. Unfortunately he was killed prematurely in a motor accident whilst on a fund-raising trip to Europe in 1921.

The hill in the Richtersveld which now bears his name produced no fabulous mineral deposits and is unimpressive to look at, but Cornell's Kop has another secret. It is inhabited by a colony of

OPPOSITE: *An aloe* (Gariepensis) *in the Jackal mountains, north of the Orange River*

strange tree aloes, *Aloe pillansii,* a rare aloe found only in the southern part of the Namib. These aloes grow to twenty feet, in a candelabra shape. In the half-light they appear like visitors from another planet, standing eerily on windswept hillsides. When I looked back as we left I almost expected to see them waving goodbye. These aloes are not alone in their other-worldly appearance. Some miles north of Cornell's Kop, near a long disused copper mine called Numeses (opened by the British explorer Sir James Alexander using Cornish miners in the 1830s), Piet led me up a barren hillside to another group of weird sentinels. 'These are "Half Mens",' he said. 'They're extremely rare, a protected species.' 'Half Mens' means half human, which accurately describes this one-legged succulent that stands about as high as a man, sometimes taller, with a bent head of green crinkled leaves. It also boasts another name, 'elephant's trunk', because apart from its similar proportions and colour its trunk is covered in hairy bracts. The scientific name is *Pachypodium namaquanum*.

There are hardly any trees in the Richtersveld, excepting the occasional riverbed stalwart, but there is a third one-legged character which is relatively common in the mountains and on the gravel plains of the southern Namib – the quiver tree. Otherwise known as the kokerboom, this single-stemmed aloe (*Aloe dichotoma*) has a light, honeycomb trunk with thin fibrous roots that cling precariously to rocky shale and debris. Its common name comes from the Bushmen's old custom of using the trunk as a quiver for their arrows. Its lightweight nature made it ideal for this purpose.

The Bushmen made use of many of the desert plants and shrubs. In the northern Namib earlier this year I was shown two other succulent shrubs, parts of which they used to make poison for their arrows. Indeed, the common name for one of these is the 'poison bush' (*Adenium boehinianum*), which, when I found it on the slopes of the Baynes Mountains, was covered in beautiful pink flowers. The Bushmen also used the poison from this plant to catch fish, poisoning the water in river pools after rain. The other more common succulent which they used is the 'bottle tree' (*Pachypodium laelii*), of which I saw several in Damaraland, one of them in flower, a rather grotesque bulbous-looking shrub.

It is now a long time since my first visit to the Namib, and since my first encounter with *Welwitschia mirabilis,* the Namib's weirdest and most wonderful plant. Described as a living fossil and a botanical enigma, Welwitschia was first discovered in south-west Angola in 1859 by the Austrian botanist Dr Friedrich Welwitsch. When Kew Gardens received specimens from the explorer Thomas Baines, the director, Sir William Hooker, wrote a special address on the plant, proclaiming it 'the most wonderful botanical discovery of the century'. My own first view of this prehistoric relative of the pine was on a foggy afternoon near the Swakop Canyon in the central Namib. At first it looked to me as though someone had left untidy heaps of leaves lying around until I noticed that there seemed to be a cohesion to these heaps. In the eerie half-light of the fog my mind wandered easily to John Wyndham's *Day of the Triffids* and other science fiction novels. They resembled enormous spiders and I found myself looking over my shoulder to see if the plants had moved while my back was turned. I realized, of course, what they must be, having been briefed before my trip, and marvelled at their ugly beauty.

The Welwitschia has two great leathery leaves, up to nine feet long, which grow from a massive turnip-like stem. As the plant gets older these leaves become frayed by the desert winds and split, giving the appearance of many leaves. The turnip-like stem is the top of a tap-root that descends

PREVIOUS PAGES: *The Richtersveld, a rugged wilderness south of the Orange River in the Cape Province*

OPPOSITE: *A dead quiver tree in the Richtersveld*

deep into the ground to suck water from below the sands. The largest specimens can stand up to six feet above the ground, with stems that measure nearly five feet in diameter. The overall plant might measure ten feet across. Such species are known to be well over a thousand years old, possibly nearer two thousand. The Welwitschia thrives in areas which receive less than an inch of rainfall a year, the secret of its survival lying not only in its tap-root but also in its long, broad leaves specially designed to absorb the fog moisture, and it grows only in the fog-belt. Until recently it was thought that pollination took place through the agency of a little red beetle, or possibly via the wind. Now it has been established that other insects are the pollinators, probably different species of wasp which carry the pollen from plant to plant on their undersides.

For many scientists the Namib is a source of endless fascination, with new revelations round every corner. Two original-minded geologists who plunged themselves into its wonders were the German refugees Henno Martin and Hermann Korn, who fled into the Namib to escape internment by the South Africans at the start of World War II. In his classic book, *The Sheltering Desert*, published after the war, Henno Martin tells the story of their camps in different parts of the Kuiseb Canyon area. These 'shelters' remain undisturbed, and in 1985 I drove from Windhoek to see them for myself. The road took me west through the Khomas Hochland, an arid, eroded landscape strewn with black boulders and outcrops of white quartz. Interestingly, the 'Hochland' is thought by some geologists to be all that remains of a vast mountain range which, millions of years ago, stood higher than the Himalayas of today. I followed the dusty road down towards the Namib through a maze of rugged ravines with frequent spectacular views of the desert ahead. It dropped steeply down below the Gamsburg, a well-known mountain landmark, before levelling out at the edge of the desert. The Namib stretched away to the horizon, and once again I felt the vastness and emptiness of this primeval world. Only the occasional quiver tree and the distant mountain ranges broke the view.

My road entered a labyrinth of rocky gullies known by the locals as the gramadullas. Zigzagging through these, I reached the Kuiseb Canyon where the two Germans and their dog, Otto, lived for more than two years. All three shelters were intact but the last I came upon was the

Namaqualand daisies in the southern Namib

*A bottle tree (*Pachypodium laelii*) in Damaraland. Parts of this tree were used by the Bushmen to make poison for their arrows*

most undisturbed and the most atmospheric. Apart from the fact that the wooden roof had collapsed, it was as if they had just walked out. According to the son-in-law of Siedentopf, the farmer who became their friend and ally, the kitchen and the table were just as they had been when Korn and Martin lived there. As I looked around the sky behind was dark and forbidding, heralding an approaching storm. I could imagine them both standing here hoping and praying that the rain would come their way, bringing with it both water and game. During the summer months of those two years the sky often threatened like this but nothing came of it. Either the clouds dissolved and dissipated or the rain fell ten miles away – a long way for them to walk for food in that terrain.

In his book Henno Martin relates how they dared not stay too long in any one place for fear of discovery, and sometimes they came across footprints in the sand which could have been made by their pursuers. At their first shelter, which they called Carp Cliff, they had a little vegetable garden in the cool depths of the canyon, until it was raided by baboons. They shot gemsbok, springbok and klipspringer for meat (when they were able to surprise them), and made their own cartridges for the shotgun. In their leisure hours they studied the rocks and the social behaviour of the animals. It was not only larger animals like zebra, gemsbok and hyena which fascinated them, but also the Namib's smaller creatures, such as beetles, spiders and lizards, who lived in the nearby dunes. They also listened to the disembodied voice of Hitler declaring war on France on a radio which they ran off the battery of their truck. The battery, in turn, was charged from a makeshift windmill they had erected nearby. After these broadcasts they often philosophized round their fire late into the night on the uncivilized nature of mankind when compared to the ways of the creatures of the wild. They were now living in a more civilized environment, they reckoned, than their fellow men. They had, however, brought with them from the 'uncivilized' world a bar of chocolate, and on Christmas Day 1940 treated themselves to one square each, giving two to Otto. Unfortunately in 1942 Hermann became ill from a vitamin deficiency and they were forced to give themselves up. Tragically, Hermann was killed in a motor accident at the end of the war.

The Namib has become known internationally in recent years for its *little* creatures. This is partly as a result of Mary Seely's work (Mary is Director of the well-known Desert Research Station at Gobabeb on the Kuiseb), and of other books and films, such as *Namib*, a beautiful film made by the wildlife cameraman David Hughes. In the *Living Sands* (the American title of Hughes' film) David caught the world's imagination with his photography of the tiny characters that live in the sands, especially the lizards and beetles. There are numerous beetles in the Namib, most of them not occurring anywhere else. On the dunes you see their little tracks criss-crossing the sand, a graphic record of the previous night's activities. At dawn they go about their business in a very determined way. I remember once at Sossusvlei hearing a distant clicking sound in the total stillness of the early morning. The sound increased and I realized that something was coming in my direction at high speed. A small black dot then appeared, moving rapidly over the sand. As it approached I saw a large beetle (*Tenebrionid*), about two inches long, with spidery legs keeping it clear from the hot sand. I could clearly hear the 'clickety-click' of its minute feet on the sand, and for

Welwitschia mirabilis, *one of the Namib's oldest plants and a distant relative of the pine, has a long tap-root to suck water from below the sands*

ABOVE: *A desert plant* (Zygophyllum sp.) *finds shelter from the scorching winds behind a small rock, which dictates its shape*

FOLLOWING PAGES: *Wild chestnut in a remote valley of the Otjihipu mountains*

a nasty moment wondered if I was going to be attacked! Fortunately in the nick of time it veered off at right angles without even slowing down. The acoustics of the desert were such that I had heard it from at least fifty yards away.

Beetles are perhaps the best known of the Namib 'detritivores' – creatures that feed on leaves, seeds and parts of plants (detritus) which are blown into the desert by the hot east winds and deposited on the leeward slipface of the dunes. Most have long legs and each has evolved its own method of survival. At dawn, for instance, when the fog rolls through the desert, *Onymacris unguicularis*, commonly known as the fog-basking beetle, struggles to the crest of a dune. Tilting his body to the wind, he stands motionless and waits. Moisture from the fog condenses on his shell and gradually trickles down to his mouth. This tiny creature has learnt to survive by drawing water from the fog, a miracle of adaptation. Later, during the heat of the day, he will lie up in the cool depths of the sand.

I also saw many lizards and geckos in the dunes whose principal prey is beetles. Once, by torchlight, I was shown the nocturnal pink and almost transparent palmatogecko, which only emerges at night. As the fog rolls through the dune this little gecko licks moisture from its lidless eyes in order to survive. Its large webbed feet enable it to burrow rapidly into the sand to escape predators like spiders and snakes, and to keep away from the hot surface sand during the day. The Namib's dune life cannot exist elsewhere and has adapted to the desert as fish have to water. Detritus in the dunes plays the same role as plankton in the sea and is therefore where the life cycle

A flightless grasshopper on the gravel plains

Lichen growing on the leeward side of a quartz chip

Lithops (ruschiorum) *on a rocky ridge near the Khumib valley, Kaokoland*

begins. Watered by the fog (dew), the wind-blown seeds and shoots take root to help support this cast of little creatures.

The lizard's most formidable predator is the sidewinder, or side-winding adder, with its peculiar style of locomotion which leaves distinctive tracks in the sand – a series of broken horizontal lines. During the daylight hours it hides up in the sand with only its eyes, conveniently located at the top of its head, protruding above the surface. It drinks by sucking fog-water droplets from its scales. Another of the sand-dune predators is the golden mole, one of the Namib's most extraordinary little animals, which is rarely seen and has only seldom been photographed. The mole swims through the sand, occasionally surfacing to grab its prey. It is virtually blind, with only rudimentary eyes, but has a highly-developed sense of hearing. Although basically an insectivore, it is also partial to the legless lizard – which swims through the sand like its predator.

The southern dune fields as they appear today are not thought to be much more than ten million years old, yet below the present dunes are many fossilized dunes, the remains of a much older Namib dating back as far as eighty million years. One of the interesting aspects of the fossilized dunes – clearly visible in several parts of the desert, notably the Tsondab area – is the evidence in them showing similar forms of life to those which we see today. Creatures like the golden mole and the legless lizard, as well as many of the beetles, were also at large in the older

The waxen stems of a Bushman's Candle (Sarcocaulon patersonii)

Wavy line, made by a legless lizard swimming beneath the sand

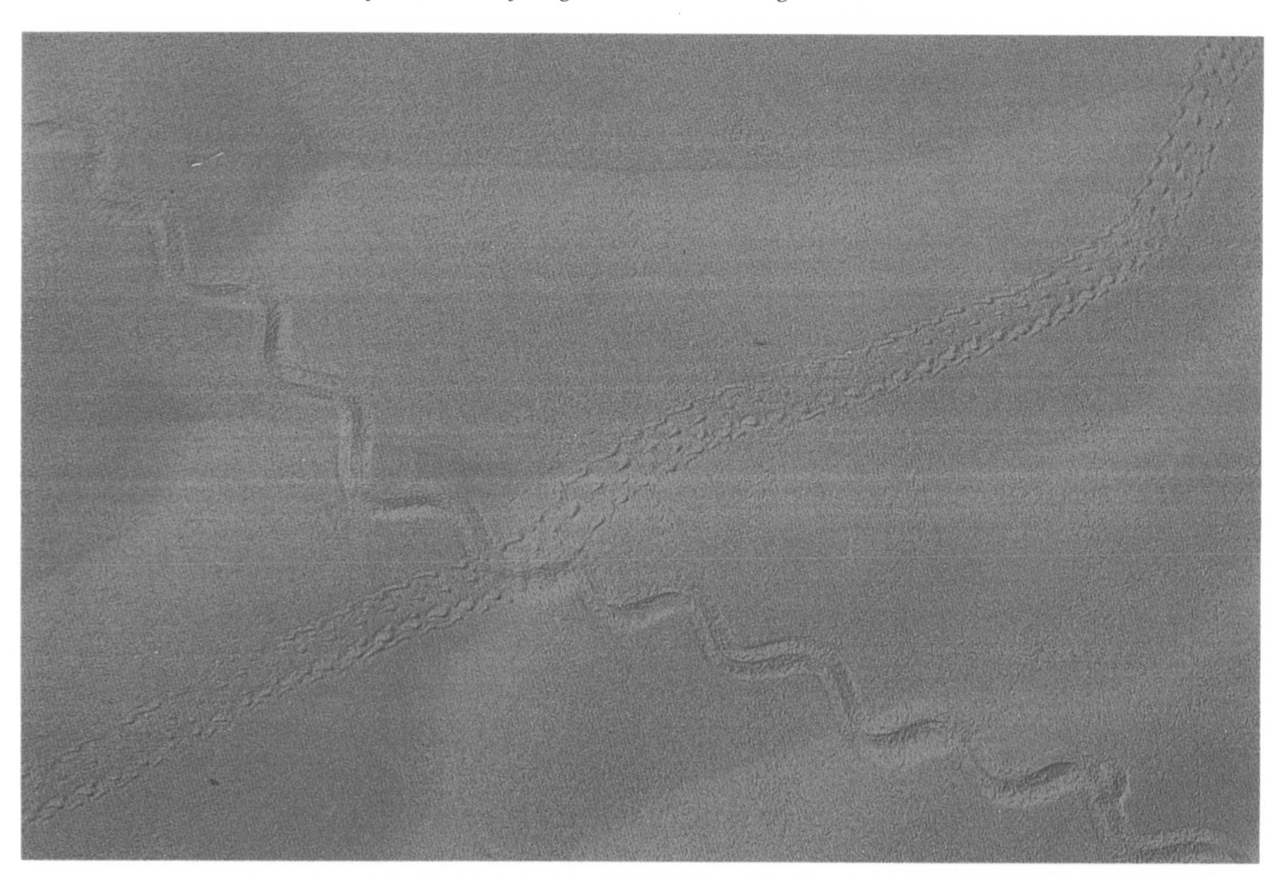

At dawn the tiny tracks of birds and beetles criss-cross the Namib sands

The Zygophyllum *shrub looks dead but will come to life after the next rainfall*

Namib. Unlike some of the world's better-known deserts, the Namib is truly a natural desert in which innumerable forms of life have had the time to evolve and adapt.

Adaptation does not only apply to the smaller creatures. The larger mammals have also performed miracles, the most spectacular examples being the desert rhino and elephant. Nowadays these animals are confined to Damaraland and Kaokoland in the northern desert, where inevitably their dwindling populations have been vulnerable to poaching. Most of the rhino live in western Damaraland between the Ugab and the Hoanib Rivers. Only a few still survive in Kaokoland north of the Hoanib, but these combined numbers represent the largest rhino population in Africa living outside a protected area.

In October 1988 I travelled for a week through western Damaraland looking for rhino with conservationist Garth Owen-Smith. A good friend from previous visits, Garth has devoted much of his recent life to conserving the wildlife of this region, particularly the rhino and elephant. I met him at his camp at World's End (Wereldsend), which could not have been more appropriately named. It is the last outpost on the map. From here on is wilderness: a vast moonscape of mountain ranges, gorges and boulder-strewn plains, stretching north to south, and traversed by riverbeds – the desert's linear oases. These riverbeds are arteries of life for the rhino, the elephant and most other desert animals.

On arrival, we set off immediately for the Uniab riverbed north-west of Palmwag so as to be there by nightfall. This was where we would begin our search. 'Search' is the operative word. Unlike elephant, rhino do not go around in herds, but in ones and twos, occasionally threes. Being low to the ground, and more or less the same colour as the rocks around them, they blend well into the landscape. I had somehow imagined that in this treeless country they would be easily seen, yet without Garth's keen eyesight and experience I would have missed most of the few we saw. We

PREVIOUS PAGES: *Slender pods decorate a Moringa* (ovalifolia) *in the north-eastern Namib*

OPPOSITE: *The palmatogecko emerges at night to hunt for beetles*

BELOW: *One of the many beetles that live in the fog-belt* – onymacris marginipennis

were also looking for perhaps fifty or sixty rhino scattered over an area of 15,000 square miles! Fortunately rhino tend to use game trails – natural routes, resembling sandy paths, which have been followed by generations of animals – and often they will use a vehicle track if there is one. In this way we could pick up their spoor and get some idea of their movements. Usually Garth was able to tell how recent the prints were, but often we would drive for miles along riverbeds, expecting any minute to come across a rhino, only to find that the tracks led up into rocky terrain where we lost the spoor. Even standing on vantage points, scouring the valleys with our binoculars, we could see nothing. Another rhino had vanished.

Perhaps our most exciting encounter was late one afternoon after another day's unsuccessful search when, scanning the broad valley along which we were driving, something unusual caught my eye. About half a mile away between two clumps of pale green euphorbia, known locally as the 'milkbush' (melkbos), there was a grey patch, rather oddly shaped. It couldn't be a tree or a bush. Could it be a rhino's head? I asked Garth what he thought and he agreed that it was worth investigating.

'We'll have to go on foot because if it is a rhino he might hear the engine and run off. What we must do is walk downwind of him and approach from there. There's virtually no cover, so we'll have to be very careful.'

These desert rhino are the highly mobile and unpredictable black rhino (*Diceros bicornis*), one of the world's most dangerous animals, and can weigh up to two tons. Fortunately such statistics were far from my mind, though, as we stalked up on what we hoped would be a desert rhino. As we approached we saw that it was indeed a rhino and there was at least one other with it.

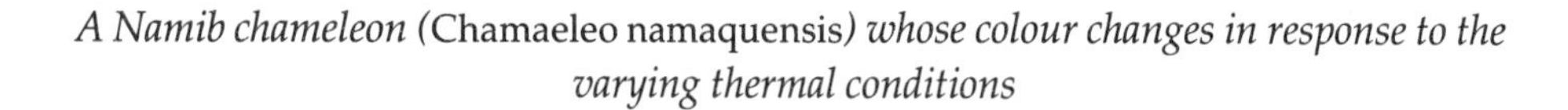
A Namib chameleon (Chamaeleo namaquensis) *whose colour changes in response to the varying thermal conditions*

Initially Garth and I were able to keep some euphorbia bushes between us and the rhino, but as we got closer we began to run out of cover. From here on we had to move extremely cautiously. Rhino have notoriously bad eyesight, yet they *can* see sudden movements and will certainly hear a stone accidentally dislodged. As a result we were carefully watching where we placed our feet, as well as keeping a wary eye on the prehistoric-looking creatures ahead of us. When we were close enough to take photographs, we stopped and slowly raised our cameras. I was worried about the sound of my shutter, which was noisier than Garth's. We could see that they had heard something and this probably made for a better picture because they appeared more alert. But it was also fairly nerve-racking. When they became used to the noise they actually relaxed a bit, and then Garth had to give a low whistle to make them alert again. Whistling at rhino is a skilled business. If you whistle too softly they do not hear you, yet if you whistle too loudly they charge. Earlier he had briefed me on how to respond in an emergency.

'If they charge and there's no cover close by, we just get down, like this.' He knelt down on one knee. 'And we might have to lie flat. The important thing is not to present a target. If we get down low they can't see us. They get confused and stop. Of course, if there's a decent bush nearby we might be able to run for it. Just watch me and do exactly what I do and you'll be OK.'

There are very few people I would trust in a situation like this, and Garth is one of them. He is very experienced and level-headed in a crisis. Seeing him standing beside me, lean and bearded, whistling at Africa's most dangerous animal, I felt surprisingly secure and was able to appreciate the remarkable spectacle in front of us. To see rhino in this type of country was truly extraordinary. Nowhere else on earth do they live in such arid surroundings, or in such rugged, hostile terrain.

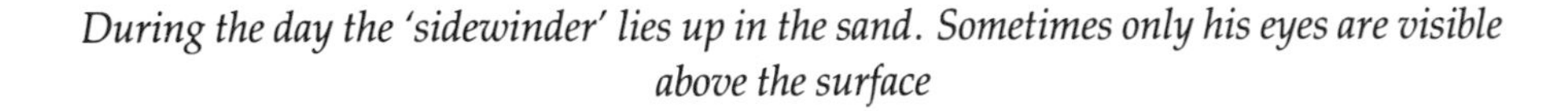

During the day the 'sidewinder' lies up in the sand. Sometimes only his eyes are visible above the surface

Jackal in the dunes

A Namib meerkat

ABOVE: *Battleur eagle in Kaokoland*

PREVIOUS PAGES: *Dwarfed by giant sand-dunes, a camel-thorn survives on subterranean moisture, Sossusvlei*

Round our camp-fires at night Garth told me about the struggle to protect the Kaokoveld's black rhino, now one of Africa's most endangered animals. 'Our biggest problem is policing this area,' Garth said. 'It's so vast and so rugged that it's practically impossible to patrol effectively. That's why we decided some time ago to involve the local people at grass-root level and this has so far paid dividends.'

When Garth says 'we', he is referring mainly to himself and two other dedicated personalities: Chris Eyre, the Government's Senior Nature Conservation Official in Kaokoland, and Blythe Loutit, a talented artist and conservationist who has devoted much of her recent life to saving the desert rhino here. With Garth and others she founded Namibia's 'Save the Rhino Fund' which is supported by several outside organizations and works in co-operation with government. Most of Blythe's time is spent driving thousands of miles alone in her Land-Rover through some of the roughest country on earth, tirelessly monitoring the rhinos' movements and their population distribution. She and Garth have built up identikit files on each of their rhino, assisted by other non-government and government staff. Blythe's husband, Rudi Loutit, is the government's Senior Conservator in charge of Damaraland and the adjoining Skeleton Coast National Park. They thus make an effective team.

FOLLOWING PAGES: *Originally created by decomposing euphorbia bushes, which contaminate the soil, or by termites which eat the grasses from below, these bare patches are scoured out by wind, creating sand circles. These circles are then invaded by harvester ants who use them as seed traps and help perpetuate their shape*

BELOW: *A group of ostriches take flight*

In 1983 Chris Eyre was stationed in Damaraland, and following the widespread poaching of the late 1970s and early 1980s, he and Garth decided on the policy of involving the local people in anti-poaching patrols and protection. These are people who live on the eastern fringes of the wilderness area. They both feel that the future hope for wildlife conservation in Africa lies with the rural communities in the areas concerned. Only by convincing them that they will benefit from the conservation of their wildlife will such animals be saved from extinction. In 1983 Chris and Garth initiated a campaign of conservation education in these areas, which resulted in the Damara and Herero tribal authorities imposing a total ban on hunting in the region. This was a major breakthrough because poachers would now be breaking tribal laws in addition to government laws. The social implications were a more serious deterrent than a spell in a government prison or the paying of fines.

In order to enforce this hunting ban, Garth, who was then Executive Officer of the Namibia Wildlife Trust, started what came to be known as the Auxiliary Game Guard System, under the auspices of the Trust. This involved the selection of local tribesmen by area headmen for appointment as game guards. The guards were thus responsible to their communities, although supervised and trained by Garth and Chris. This system has to date been so successful that the rhino population in Damaraland has actually increased since its instigation, the only black rhino population in Africa to have increased during the same period.

Watching Garth telling his story, his bearded face lit by the flickering firelight, it occurred to me that Namibia was fortunate to have such dedicated people to serve it. For many years he trod a lonely path, often not knowing where his next meal would come from. Ostracized by the authorities, whom he had embarrassed with certain disclosures, he was forced to spend long periods away from his family. He knew he had to look after the desert elephant and rhino in Damaraland, but at the same time he also had to keep his children at school. Between 1984 and 1987 he lived alone at World's End without a radio or telephone, supervising the Game Guard system. Had he not done so it would no doubt have disintegrated and the last remaining elephant and rhino might have disappeared. His friend and supporter, Chris Eyre, had been temporarily transferred to the south of Namibia and did not return until 1987, so during this period he was completely on his own.

The next day we drove on, heading west towards the unfenced border of the Skeleton Coast Park. In the late morning we came across a herd of giraffe looking absurdly exposed on a desolate mountainside, totally devoid of vegetation. With effortless ease they negotiated the rocky slopes, stopping right at the top of a mountain pass on the skyline to look back at us. Shortly afterwards Garth suddenly halted and scrutinized the valley below with his binoculars.

'Two rhino,' he said, 'and they're heading for that patch of bush at the bottom of the valley. They'll probably lie up there during the heat of the day, so we should be able to take a look at them.'

Driving as quietly as possible, we approached to within quarter of a mile of the thicket and then continued on foot. We could now see one of the rhino asleep under a tree, though the second was not in evidence. Before taking any risks we had to know exactly where the other one was, so we cautiously explored the thicket from a respectable distance, and after a while spotted the second one lying under another tree about a hundred yards from the first. We would now know where not

PREVIOUS PAGES: *Gemsbok in the Koichab valley*

OPPOSITE: *'We came across a herd of giraffe looking absurdly exposed on a desolate mountainside. . . . With effortless ease they negotiated the rocky slopes'*

ABOVE: *Black rhino in north-western Damaraland. Being low to the ground and more or less the same colour as the rocks around them, rhino blend in well with this landscape*

PREVIOUS PAGES: *'Initially Garth and I were able to keep some euphorbia bushes between us and the rhino, but as we got closer we began to run out of cover'*

OPPOSITE: *'For a split second I knelt and took two photographs . . . and then we were both running full tilt for the tree, and it felt good to be running'*

to run and could keep one eye on him while photographing his companion. The problem with this plan was that the first rhino, a magnificent animal, was very much asleep and looking rather unimpressive, on his side, in the shade of a tamarisk.

'If you're going to get the picture you want, we're going to have to wake him, I'm afraid there's no alternative,' said Garth.

With that he picked up a small stone and, to my horror, threw it with such accuracy that it hit the animal on the rump. In a split second he was on his feet, nearly two tons of him on full alert. Meanwhile we stood motionless next to a bush about thirty yards away, looking to see what he would do next. Garth then nodded very slowly, indicating that he thought I could safely take one or two pictures. The rhino snorted when he heard my shutter going, and pawed the ground like a bull. Should I take another shot? Nothing ventured, nothing gained, so I took another. The rhino charged – an impressive sight. Garth indicated downwards with his hand and knelt on one knee, his head held low. I did the same, my body charged with adrenalin, heart thumping like a generator. Every instinct told me to run like hell, but we knelt there dead still, watching him like hawks. Ten yards away he stopped, sniffing and snorting, obviously confused. He sniffed from side to side and then withdrew a few yards while facing us. Quick as a flash Garth was up and ran behind the nearby bush with me close on his heels. We heard another snort and saw dust but then silence followed. Thank God.

'Next time we show ourselves, if he charges, you could try and grab a shot before we run to that tree over there. Up to you, but only a split second mind you, don't delay.'

That bit of advice was, of course, unnecessary, though appreciated. Slowly we moved out on the other side of our bush and there he was still looking in our direction. I took another photograph and he came for us, dust flying, two tons of rhino bearing down on us. For a split second I knelt and took two photos. I saw Garth doing the same, and then we were both running full tilt for the tree and it felt good to be running. We reached the tree and when the rhino had lost us he stopped again and withdrew a few yards. We breathed again. Obviously all this emotion was also affecting the poor rhino, because we then saw him trot off briskly up the mountainside beyond, a truly prehistoric sight against that red lava shale. The second rhino had also got to its feet now, and a few minutes later followed his friend up the mountain. Soon both were lost to sight and we sat exhausted on a tree trunk. Rarely have I had a more exciting half hour. What would have happened if either of us had tripped? It didn't bear thinking about.

I had first met Garth in 1985 when I was photographing desert elephant for an article on the Namib. My own interest in these special animals stemmed from an expedition I had joined in 1981, the 'Kaokoland Desert Elephant Expedition', led by Clive Walker, who was then Chairman of the Endangered Wildlife Trust of Southern Africa (EWT). At that time the world's attention had just been focused on the plight of these animals, following press reports of widespread poaching in the area by high-ranking officers of the South African Defence Force (SADF) and senior government officials.

Some of the Damara and Hereros had also climbed on to the poaching bandwagon, and the western elephant population had now been reduced from an estimated three hundred in 1970 to a mere seventy animals in 1981. At the same time excitement had been raised by a statement from a South African university professor, who claimed to have measured an elephant rub mark on a tree at thirteen foot six inches from the ground. This would have made a world record – the tallest elephant in Africa. As it happened, there had already been other unconfirmed reports that the desert elephant were taller than ordinary savannah elephant, and also had bigger feet. So now an expedition had been mounted, first to establish the extent of the poaching and to see how many animals remained, and second to try and establish if these elephant were indeed taller, and whether they were a separate subspecies that was about to become extinct. After all, the presence of elephant in this area was very much in conflict with the prevailing concept of elephant habitat requirements.

Soon after arriving at the expedition's camp on the northern banks of the Hoanib west of Sesfontein (six springs), a total of eight elephant carcasses were counted within a radius of a quarter of a mile of the camp. Among other horrors which I photographed on that trip were carcasses where the heads had been cut through with chain-saws to remove the tusks. We had also, in fact, already heard that helicopters had been used by white poachers. In the late 1980s, the then Commissioner-General for the Indigenous Peoples of South West Africa had admitted that he had used SADF helicopters to hunt both elephant and the rare and endangered black-faced impala in Kaokoland. (In 1984 the very same man apparently made a serious proposal to offer Western European nations dumping facilities for nuclear waste in Kaokoland.)

The most important objective of the expedition was to dart a large bull so that detailed measurements could be made and tests carried out. The expedition followed a five-and-a-half-year Ph.D. study conducted by a South African wildlife student, Slang Viljoen, on the Hoanib River population, ('Slang' means snake, a name given to him after he was bitten as a child.) During this period Slang had amassed a considerable amount of important data, but no elephant had yet been darted. Our first problem now was to find the right elephant, and the second to approach close enough to get a shot with a dart gun.

For the first four days we drove many bone-rattling miles up and down that riverbed looking for elephant, but as soon as we approached to within five hundred yards they were off, and all we ever saw was their dust. These animals had been badly poached over the years and were understandably nervous. After a while Clive started using his aeroplane to do early morning searches for elephant, whereupon, having found a likely bull, he would land and we would set off post-haste in the vehicles for the place he had seen from the air. Only on our last day did we finally achieve success. Driving to the target area we left our vehicles and continued on foot, following Slang, who was running ahead with the dart gun. We saw him disappear in some bush and suddenly we heard a shot. Next we were treated to the spectacle of a huge elephant running fast down the riverbed, with Slang in hot pursuit. We ran as fast as we could and were just in time to see the bull slow down and sink back onto its haunches.

'We've got to get him onto his side,' someone shouted, so we all began to push the huge animal from the side with all our strength until suddenly he went over with a great 'flump'. The experts immediately got busy, there being no time to lose. While Clive poured gallons of water from jerrycans over his exposed ear (an elephant's cooling system is in its ear – if the ear is not moving it can easily overheat due to its large surface area), others were busy measuring his feet, his teeth to indicate age, and his height. There was someone performing 'rear-end' tests and another person fitting a radio collar round his neck. The prescribed half hour was soon up and the vet told everyone to get clear while he administered the antidote. Within seconds the great bull was rolling and thrashing around tyring to get on his feet. We were all clustered on the rocks above snapping away with our cameras, feeling a little nervous about how he would react. One more roll and he was on

Footprint of a desert elephant in the Hoanib riverbed

his feet, wheeling round to look at us just above him. We looked down in silence, anxiously wondering what he was thinking. As if to answer, he gave a rolling toss of his great head, 'To hell with you all, I don't know who you are and I'm not interested.' In no time he was off across the riverbed, vanishing into the bush. Only the dust betrayed where he had gone.

One of the main findings of that expedition was that desert elephant are probably no taller than other elephant in Africa. Our bull only measured about eleven feet at the shoulder, for instance, which is not exceptionally tall for an elephant, just a respectable height. The reason why they looked so tall at that time was probably the thinness of their legs, which gave them a lean, gangly appearance. In 1981 the Kaokoveld had already been through years of drought so it was small wonder that they were thin. On that trip I remember seeing abandoned Himba (nomadic Hereros) huts and the twisted carcasses of their cattle lying by the riverbed. At that stage the drought had already claimed eight thousand of the Himba cattle and the people themselves had moved inland, abandoning the weaker beasts to their fate.

It seems strange to talk about drought in a desert, but the fact is that desert ecologies are more sensitive and marginal than normal ones. If their tiny rainfall fails them for consecutive years, thousands of plants and creatures will die. In this particular drought, which lasted from 1977 to 1982, more than eighty per cent of the large population of Kaokoveld plains mammals, like springbok and gemsbok, are thought to have died. Yet, despite some press reports at the time, Slang Viljoen later wrote that not one desert elephant had died as a result of the drought. They were fully adapted to the desert. Most of those that died perished from poachers' bullets, or were destroyed in some other way by man. The extent of their adaptation was clearly demonstrated by their low water intake, unofficially estimated at a tenth of that of a savannah elephant during lean times. Unlike most plains animals, elephant, in common with rhino and giraffe, are mainly browsers, feeding on riverine foliage and palm nuts, but elephant and giraffe have the extra advantage of height (rhino prefer coarser food like the branches and twigs of terminalia bushes). In times of drought they have learnt to survive exclusively on the riverine vegetation such as mopane, wild tamarisk and ana trees (acacias), as well as the luxury fruit of the river green-thorn, to which they are especially partial. Many of these trees will die in a long drought but some will survive, and so, therefore, do the elephants, who depend on these riverine oases. It is also possible that the experts who suggested the subspecies theory may themselves have underestimated the extraordinary versatility of the elephant, one of the world's most intelligent mammals.

The long drought broke in 1982, and by the time I met up with Garth in 1985 both rhino and elephant cows had been dropping calves. An elephant's gestation period is twenty-two months – during the drought they had instinctively stopped breeding. At the same time, there had been virtually no poaching so there had been a definite improvement in numbers. Garth offered to show me the changes in the country since my 1981 visit, so we drove north from World's End to valleys which I remembered as moonscapes, now covered in golden grass. In one of these we came across a breeding herd of elephant in a bushy riverbed, about twenty of them quietly browsing. Leaving the vehicle three hundred yards away we approached on foot. It was nearly midday and the breeze in our direction was barely perceptible. We could tell from their motionless silence that they had heard something, probably the Land-Rover when we stopped, and were now listening intently. They could not smell us or they would already have been off. Cautiously we approached to within

OPPOSITE: *Every year the elephant come down the Hoanib riverbed to visit water-holes in the western dune fields*

twenty-five yards, keeping some bushes between them and us. From this distance I could clearly see how much weight they had gained since the coming of the rains. In particular their legs looked much less lanky. Reading my thoughts Garth whispered, 'Now you can understand why people thought these elephant were taller.'

He had hardly spoken when the elephant wheeled round to face us. Perhaps they had heard us talking or maybe the wind had changed a fraction. Whatever the cause pandemonium broke loose. There is something blood-chilling about the scream of an enraged elephant. The three leaders charged, and we ran. 'They're really coming,' yelled Garth. 'Faster if you can.' We ran faster, vaulting over rocks, no longer trying to hide the noise of our feet on stones and twigs. The elephant had us in view now, recognizing us as their most hated enemies – yet for some reason they stopped. They had seen us off and we were more than lucky to get away so lightly. An elephant can run at thirty miles an hour or more. If they had persisted there would have been no hope of reaching the Land-Rover. Fortunately they had been content to give us a fright.

Round the fire that night Garth talked about the elephant's mastery of the environment. 'These elephant have an incredible knowledge of the resource distribution within their area. I have seen them set off on a fifty-mile walk to a water-hole they haven't drunk at in years, yet they go there unerringly, always by the shortest possible route.'

Both the desert elephant and the mountain zebra will dig in riverbeds to reach underground water, but with their superior strength and size the elephant can dig deeper than the zebra. I remember seeing holes dug by elephant in 1981, watching them dip their trunks into the cool, sandy depths to suck up precious water – a practice which not only enables them to survive here but also helps many other animals to obtain water.

'In other words,' said Garth, 'they keep the water-holes open. If they are poached out, all the other animals will have to leave or perish as well. They are the kingpins of a very fragile ecology.'

There are also other vital ways in which they contribute to the desert ecology. For instance, they eat foliage with hard seed pods that soften when digested, thus becoming available in the animals' dung as a potential food for game birds. In addition tests have shown that acacia seeds digested by elephant have a forty-five per cent better chance of germination than if they fall to the ground directly. Continuous browsing by the elephant also keeps the riverbed vegetation down to a level which is accessible to smaller feeders.

'When we consider the fate of these desert giants we tend to overlook the bigger, broader issues,' said Garth. 'When the elephant goes, a whole world goes with him, one that took thousands of years to evolve.'

PREVIOUS PAGES: *'The vet administered the antidote and within seconds the great elephant was rolling and thrashing, trying to get up on to his feet. Meanwhile we stood clustered on the rocks above, wondering what he would do'*

OPPOSITE: *Worn smooth by centuries of elephants that have rubbed their bellies on its cool surfaces, a rock bears testimony to the great herds that once frequented this valley*

CHAPTER THREE

Ocean Sands

The Namib coast offers great contrasts – contrasts of scenery, contrasts of wildlife, contrasts of climate. To cross the sand desert and arrive at the Atlantic with thousand-foot dunes descending dramatically to the blue-green ocean is to be present at a spectacular and unforgettable meeting of extremes.

Fresh from the Antarctic, the Benguela current flows north to the southern tip of Africa, whence it is deflected up the west coast as far as Namibe (Mossamedes) in Angola. At this point it suddenly swings west, blending with a warmer equatorial current, heading out towards South America. When the current first flows north from Antarctica it brings vast shoals of fish with it, and thereby sea-birds in their thousands. The beaches and rocky promontories also host huge colonies of seals and smaller numbers of jackass penguins, which feed on the fish. Running south-west from Angra Fria towards South America is a sub-oceanic ridge, which forms a natural trap for plankton carried north by the Benguela. It is this richness of plankton, sometimes called 'nutrient soup', which accounts for the profusion of fish and thus of sea-birds, seals and penguins. Here on the coast these predators are joined by tropical animals like hyenas, jackals, and even lions which stalk the beach, preying on the Antarctic creatures. Occasionally desert elephant make a brief appearance on this surrealist stage. All are guests of the Benguela, making this shore and this desert unique. A visit to the forbidden coast on a beautiful day evokes special feelings, but when the wind changes and the weather turns, the scene can switch from heaven to hell. Oven-hot winds from the interior, gusting up to sixty miles an hour or more, blow the sand horizontally across the desert, filling eyes, nose, mouth and hair with sand, stinging your face, getting into your cameras and lenses, and blotting out all your tracks. Experiencing one of these desert storms plunges you into another extreme. There are also nights, camping out under the stars when the fog creeps in. The Benguela fog is ice-cold, clammy and bleak. It soaks through your sleeping-bag and blankets and changes the fun and glamour of outdoor life into a spartan ordeal. I remember squatting, shivering and miserable, by tiny piles of damp wood, striking match after match in my attempts to get fires going in such conditions. I can also remember waking at dawn with ice in my hair.

One of the most exciting trips I have made to this coast was my Sylvia Hill safari in 1986. Sylvia Hill is a marble mountain surrounded by dunes on a remote stretch of the diamond coast between Luderitz and Walvis Bay. In June that year I was writing an article on the Namib for the *Smithsonian* magazine, and was granted a special permit from the diamond authorities (Consolidated Diamond Mines of South West Africa) to visit Sylvia Hill in the company of two Nature Conservators from the Department of Nature Conservation, and an assistant.

In order to reach this part of the coastline we had to cross the southern dune sea from east to west, negotiating some of the highest dunes in the world, a seemingly impossible feat in vehicles. The Nature Conservation authorities laid on two four-wheel-drive Landcruisers with special tyres, 200 gallons of fuel and an HF (high frequency) radio. Their staff drove the vehicles, one driver being Chris Eyre, who was then working in southern Namibia, and the other a man called Bassie Theron. The fourth member of our team was their Nama assistant, Dirk. Chris and I had already shared one trip together, and I could not have wished for a better guide and companion. As usual he was

OPPOSITE: *Wild coastline north of Spencer Bay*

accompanied by Jason, his intrepid fox-terrier, who shares his sleeping-bag at night (but who gets bored during the small hours and moves to mine, which always makes Chris a bit jealous; 'disloyal, bloody dog,' he mutters, and lights up another pipe).

Approaching from the east, we drove into the desert at a point south-east of Duwisib (a property formerly owned by a German baron, von Wolf, see Chapter Five) and entered the diamond area, otherwise known as the Sperrgebiet or 'forbidden area'. Vast tracts of desert were closed off to the outside world in 1908, following the discovery of diamonds. These remain closed to this day, though much of the northern diamond area has now been designated a 'conservation area'. Nothing has really changed except the reasons for the closure. The diamonds themselves only occur near the coast, but the forbidden area includes most of the low-lying desert between the beach and the escarpment seventy miles inland. In this way a buffer zone has been created to keep out the diamond thieves. You have to be a brave man to enter illegally in search of diamonds. Many 'adventurers' must have perished, and occasionally their bleached bones are uncovered by the shifting sands. Yet people do take the risk, especially in the south, and some may get away with it, though not easily from what the diamond security chief once told me. From a conservation point of view the Sperrgebiet has been a success, preserving this part of the Namib in its untouched form for the greater part of this century. CDM (Consolidated Diamond Mines) have also played an important conservation role in recent years. Today mining only takes place further south near the Orange River where the diamonds are bigger and more economic to mine.

Ahead of us the stark cliffs of the Awasib range towered impressively above the gravel plains, and we stopped in a valley between two mountains to let our tyres down in preparation for the dunes beyond. For dune driving, your tyres must be so soft that they wobble when you kick them. While the experts supervised this delicate operation, I climbed among huge granite boulders, the surfaces of which were badly flaked due to a process known as 'exfoliation'. Because of the extremes of temperature in the southern Namib, the surfaces of the granite crack and fall away in flakes, like the exterior of a croissant. Hannibal used the knowledge of this phenomenon when taking his elephants over the Alps long ago. He built fires beneath the boulders, which then disintegrated and so could be moved away by hand.

With suitably wobbly tyres our desert convoy set off, watched from a safe distance by a herd of gemsbok as we climbed into the first dune fields. The fields on the eastern side of the desert are rough going, consisting of hard ridges, hollows and grassy tussocks round which the sand has drifted. There is no direct route through, and no alternative but to weave your way through the labyrinth, hoping that you do not get stuck in a hidden hollow. It is folly to drive too fast, and a mistake to drive too slowly, but Chris was experienced. After an uncomfortable hour, the tussocks became fewer and we were into an area of bigger dunes with purer, looser sand to drive on. Ahead now were the Hauchab mountains, which we skirted before crossing a large pan about a mile long. At the edge, to my amazement, I saw an ancient bulldozer with a trailer.

'It broke down here in the 1940s, in the days when they were still mining diamonds at Saddle Hill,' said Chris. 'As far as I remember, the bulldozer was taking a load of water drums and other equipment to the mining settlement at the time. Parts for the bulldozer were unobtainable then, so it had to be abandoned along with the trailer.'

West of the pan the desert began in earnest and we selected a 'dune street' which we hoped

OPPOSITE: *Jackal tracks in the forbidden diamond area near the Skeleton Coast*

FOLLOWING PAGES: *One of our vehicles dwarfed by the desert landscape*

would lead us to Sylvia Hill. In this part of the Namib, the dunes have formed a series of diagonal, parallel ridges with valleys in between known as dune streets. If you select the right street, it can take you a long way and the going can be relatively easy. In this case we followed one for several miles, averaging between five and ten miles per hour, until we found our way blocked by massive transverse dunes rising like mountains ahead of us. Clearly we had not chosen the right street. So we stopped and did a 'recce' on foot. From the top of the nearby ridge it looked as if we should be in the street further north which, unlike ours, appeared to be a 'through street'. The difficulty was how to get there, so we split up and explored in different directions until I saw Chris gesticulating in the distance. By the look of it he had found a possible route, so we returned to the vehicles only to discover that his Landcruiser was totally bogged down. The more he tried to get it out, the deeper it sank, until it was up to the axles. There was nothing for it but to dig the cruiser out, clearing the sand from under the chassis and digging a channel for the tyres to ride in. It was an hour's work, with the noon sun blazing down, but with four of us we got her out and, before long, successfully followed Chris's route to the next dune street.

Half an hour later we found that we could now see the top of Sylvia Hill on the horizon at the end of our street: we were dead on course. In the afternoon light the dunes took on a rich colour. Topping a rise we disturbed a big male gemsbok, who thundered up the dune to our right with sand flying from his hooves, stopping near the top to look back at us. Standing there with the sunlight glinting on his great horns he looked magnificent, the king of the wilderness.

ABOVE: *The vital thing is to line up straight, or your vehicle may slew sideways and roll*

OPPOSITE: *'It was alarming to think that we were about to take vehicles down these precipitous slopes; yet down we went, swimming without control through the loose sand'*

The climax of the day was cresting the final dunes and seeing the ocean far below. Up here the wind was blowing strongly, so we set up camp in the lee of a dune, arranging our vehicles at right angles to each other with the tarpaulin rigged to prevent the wind from coming under them. Later Chris and I went for an evening walk to look at some old hut circles on the exposed terraces once inhabited by hunter-gatherers, while Bassie and Dirk went down to the beach to fish for our supper. Sylvia Hill is, in fact, a marble mountain, half engulfed by sand and sculpted by the wind into extraordinary shapes and textures. The marble itself is composed of multicoloured rock – cream, rust brown, gold and claret red – and the prevailing south-west winds have fashioned it over the centuries, creating an exquisite grain. On these exposed surfaces are a number of rock circles resembling mini Stonehenges, which would once have anchored huts or shelters made from driftwood or whale bones. It was extraordinary to think of prehistoric hunter-gatherers, formerly known as Strandlopers, managing to survive in such a bleak and isolated place on shellfish and water carried from inland in ostrich eggshells (see p. 153).

Before sunset I climbed onto a headland, which was part of the marble mountain. The sinking sun laid a fiery path across the pale green ocean, with skeins of cormorants dipping and skimming, silhouetted in effortless flight. Below me lazy rollers collided with the cliffs, sending plumes of golden spray to meet the sea-birds, and beyond, above a misty beach, giant dunes glowed like the embers of a dying fire. There was now not a breath of wind, and sitting round our fire we heard

the ghostly motor of a trawler far out to sea, its lights obscured by an offshore fog-bank. Later the moon rose above the fog-bank, illuminating incoming breakers like silver foil.

We woke to a perfect dawn. Mist hung over the bay and before sunrise, while the others slept, I climbed up the hill past the stone circles to the top of a dune. On a cliff nearby were cormorants nesting, diving periodically from their perch to join their friends above the waves. In the windless calm of the early morning, the ocean heaved in a moody, hazy swell, merging imperceptibly with the sky on the horizon. Against the pastel backdrop flocks of birds soared and dived in a demonstration of ultimate freedom, tiny dots over the ocean vastness. All around me the marble mountain was on fire with incredible colours, moving from the golden red colour of dunes to the creamy yellow and burgundy of the eroded slabs of marble just below my sandy tower. The sun was catching the summit of Sylvia Hill and the highest dunes, as well as the crests of the breakers out to sea. Never have I seen such intoxicating beauty. Sitting there, looking out over the bay, I felt totally at peace and harmony with the world, an inseparable part of something magic and wonderful.

Meanwhile, in a little valley below, a wisp of smoke announced that coffee was ready, so I made my way back for breakfast. Our camp was a hive of activity, and Chris and Bassie were discussing the next stage of our journey. Our plan now was to descend to the beach and drive north at low tide, running the gauntlet between breakers and dunes for thirty-five miles. Our objective was to reach the spring near Meob Bay, and then to look for some ghost settlements I had

PREVIOUS PAGES: *Sylvia Hill, our marble mountain on the diamond coast*

OPPOSITE: *Weathered slab of marble at Sylvia Hill*

BELOW: *A rare succulent endemic to this area,* Jensenobotrya lossowiana, *on the windswept summit of Dolphin Head at Spencer Bay*

PREVIOUS PAGES 92–3: *Dusk on the beach below Sylvia Hill*

PREVIOUS PAGES 94–5: *Sandwich Bay, where the Namib's largest dunes descend to the Atlantic*

photographed from the air the previous year (see Chapter Six). Hemmed in by huge dunes these settlements, abandoned by the Germans after World War I, are only really accessible from the beach on the western side.

Our first challenge was to get down to the beach, so we headed back inland and picked up a dune street which led us to a pass further north, about fifteen hundred feet above the sea. Standing up here, far above the ocean, it was extraordinary to realize that we were on a sand-dune and not a mountain. It was also alarming to think that we were about to take vehicles down these precipitous sand slopes – but down we went until we reached the top of the final slipface that drops three hundred feet to the beach. From the top I watched Chris take his Landcruiser down, swimming without control through the sand. 'The vital thing,' said Chris to a terrified Bassie, 'is to line up straight or the vehicle will slew sideways and roll.' But Chris was a star and Bassie, who two years later lost a vehicle in these dunes, I am told, followed successfully in Chris's tracks. We were safely down on the beach and now, while the tide was out, we had to drive for our lives along the hard sand. I remember sunlight glinting off wet sand, pebbles, gravel and shells as we sped along below the dunes – it was a dazzling morning.

We drove northward in convoy between the surf and the base of the dunes. The sky was a brilliant blue and the ocean an emerald green, while high in the dunes, above a layer of mist, the fossil shellbeds appeared as patches of drifted snow. Ahead of us colonies of cormorants and

ABOVE: *A colony of great white pelicans resting on a sandy spit between fishing forays in Sandwich Bay lagoon*

waders took to the air, returning to the beach when we had passed. Sections of the beach were stained with garnet sand as if a drunken giant had spilt claret from a glass in the sky. At one point we stopped to look at a strange bird, sitting all by itself at the foot of the dunes.

'What on earth is a barn owl doing in a place like this?' asked Chris.

'Having a seaside holiday on the Skeleton Coast,' I replied, 'living on seafood and lizards.'

It sounded far-fetched, yet what other explanation could there be? Had he been blown off course by a severe south-wester? That was equally unlikely.

Half an hour later we reached an obstacle marked on our map as 'Black Rock'. At first sight it looked impassable, but perhaps we would be able to dig a path for the vehicles on the dune side of the rocks. Out came the shovels and we set to work with a vengeance. Time was not on our side. Already the tide was starting to come in and we still had a long way to go. Fortunately our efforts were rewarded, and on we drove, only to find that this was the beginning of a bad patch. Soon both vehicles were becoming 'bogged' repeatedly. One moment the surface was firm, and the next we were wallowing in heavy wet sand, engine screaming, trying to break free. Sometimes we were able to dig the sand away and successfully smooth out a get-away path. At others we were forced to resort to the winch, using the first vehicle to pull out the second. The bad sand was followed by a bed of sharp rocks, and in this case we shovelled on a layer of sand to protect our tyres. Still further we found our way blocked by a barrier of rock. Try as we might, we could not get by, so instead we found a route up the dunes from where we climbed into a valley, returning to the beach further on, thus circumventing the problem.

That evening we camped at Meob Bay, and while Chris and Bassie went fishing for supper, I explored the old settlement of Meob. The bay had once been a source of supply to the northern diamond fields, and shallow draft 'whalers' took people ashore from the steamers. Two of these boats still lay on the beach, abandoned long ago. It was a wild scene, the wind catching the golden crests of the foaming breakers, blowing them sideways to form a mist over the dark blue sea. A narrow-gauge railway led down to the beach, and I found several old rail-buggies lying on their sides. I recognized an object in the distance as one of the water barrels that was used to bring drinking water from Luderitz. These huge wooden barrels were pulled through the dunes behind camels or mules on an axle, as though pulling a garden roller through the desert. Robustly built, some are well preserved to this day. Near the barrel was an empty house, whose timber walls had survived generations of storms. Judging from the sand-blasted bottles lying around, I guessed that this had once been an inn. Traders and fortune seekers would have stayed here, before departing on their trek to the diamond fields.

Further up the coast, about eighty miles north of Meob, is Sandwich Bay, where a long spit of sand has created a beautiful lagoon, a haven for tens of thousands of migratory and local birds. This is where the Namib's highest and most majestic dunes drop to the Atlantic. In April 1989 I spent a

OPPOSITE: *The brown hyena is mainly nocturnal and lives on fish and seals washed up on the beach*

BELOW: *Barn owl on the Skeleton Coast, an unexpected visitor*

few days at Sandwich, having driven the fifty miles south from Walvis Bay. There is a little beach hut, tucked away in a thicket of reeds, which is reserved for the use of occasional scientists and nature conservators, and here I was allowed to camp. To get to it by vehicle you have to drive through the lagoon at low tide, a nerve-racking experience if you happen to be alone, as I was. Depending upon the offshore winds, there are high low tides and low low tides, and the afternoon when I drove across was an example of a high low tide. I waded the route several times in advance, until eventually I realized that the tide was coming in again. It was obviously not going to get any shallower, and if I was to get across I would have to 'go for it', which I did. I managed, but the water came well above the level of the bumper and the wheel hubs, and I consider myself lucky to have got through. If I had got stuck the tide would have come in and, since there was no help within fifty miles, I would have lost the vehicle. Fortunately on the return trip the tide was lower.

That evening I climbed into the dunes before the fog came in, and watched flocks of flamingos and pelicans flighting in at sunset. A fantastic colour in the fading light, the surface of the dunes was etched with intricate patterns, caused by recent rainfall I was later told. Soon the fog swallowed the setting sun and I descended to the relative shelter and comfort of my hut. Thanks to the tall reeds, I was protected from the wind and perfectly warm. Nearby was a well where I drew fresh water, using a pulley and a bucket, and I made a small fire outside to cook on. In the distance, I could hear the ocean surf and the occasional howl of a jackal. I felt a million miles from anywhere.

The following morning I discovered that something, a rat I think, had got into my coolbox, which I had left on the bonnet of the Landcruiser (out of harm's way). Whatever it was had eaten the bread, leaving a long dark hair behind. The mist was beginning to clear, so after breakfast I set off south on foot between the dunes and the sea, hoping to find an old shipwreck I had once spotted from the air. As the mist broke, shafts of sunlight poked through, lighting up ethereal patches of dune far above me and a group of vivid white egrets, feeding on the beach below. A great white pelican on the shore watched my approach uneasily, and finally took flight with several strokes of his mighty wings. Rounding the headland, I came across fresh gemsbok and brown hyena tracks, but saw no sign of either animal. The brown hyena is a strange looking beast with a long shaggy coat, which makes you think at first sight that it is a dog. Being mainly nocturnal, you rarely see it in good light. It is quite common along the Namib coast, and also in parts of the Kalahari in Botswana. The brown hyenas of the Namib appear to have shaggier coats than their Kalahari cousins, which they certainly need here.

Half a mile on, I came to a narrow lagoon where the water seemed very turbulent, until I realized that a shoal of mullet had been trapped as the tide went out. As I walked up to the water's edge they all congregated in front of me, jumping and swimming in circles at high speed. It was as though they were saying, 'Look at us! See what a great time we're having!' They were so close to the surface that I had a clear view of them. Some must have weighed three or four pounds. It was rather like being at a fish farm at feeding time. I was obviously not alone in my observations, because at the other end of this lagoon was a colony of at least a hundred great white pelicans, preening themselves and occasionally making fishing forays.

It was a crystal clear day without a breath of wind, the sea a deep turquoise, and the dunes a reddish gold. Out in the bay were sandy spits and islands with more pelicans, as well as cormorants and large congregations of waders. According to Walvis Bay ornithologist, Tony Williams, most of the waders migrate annually between here and, believe it or not, Siberia. Sandwich is one of only four havens on the whole Namib coast for so-called 'wetland' birds (the other three being Luderitz, Walvis Bay and Bahia dos Tigres in Angola), and attracts those long-distance migrants in their thousands. The muddy pools of the Siberian tundra are ideal summer breeding grounds for them. As the snow begins to melt, they start breeding and their fluffy chicks feed on the mosquito and fly larvae which abound up there. Time is limited though. Within three months the pools freeze again, and tens of thousands of birds begin their long flight to the shores of Southern Africa. The little birds can only store enough 'fuel' for relatively small hops of about two or three hundred miles at a time, so they stop off on the way to refuel. Of these waders the most common are curlew sandpipers and sanderlings, but turnstones and grey plovers also arrive in great numbers. The little stint flies back and forth to Siberia twice a year, which is not bad for a bird that weighs only twenty-five grammes.

Further south, I came to a part of the bay where the big dunes dropped steeply into deep blue water, leaving only a narrow shelf for me to walk along. Two sand sharks swam past only feet away as I skirted the dunes, and after a while I saw the *Eagle* at the back of an old inlet, half buried in the sand. I had first seen these ribs and spars protruding from the sand when flying to Conception Bay in 1985. At that time I was told that they were the remains of an old Portuguese man-of-war that had foundered here in the late 1800s. I have since discovered from Gunter von Schumann, the Namibian shipwreck enthusiast, that they are actually those of the *Eagle*, a barque which was wrecked in 1861, having originally been built in America in the 1830s where she was christened the

OPPOSITE: *Evening in the dunes at Sandwich Bay. The strange pattern on the sand may have been caused by a freak shower of rain*

FOLLOWING PAGES: *Large colony of gannets and cormorants on the coast of Namaqualand, where sea-birds gather in their thousands to feed on the shoals of fish brought north by the cold Benguela current*

ABOVE: *Flamingoes flying in formation*

OPPOSITE: *Massed flamingoes over the lagoon at Walvis Bay*

Jefferson. According to von Schumann, she was one hundred and thirty-four feet long, twenty-four feet wide and weighed two hundred and forty-four tons. She had a poop and a figurehead, which was latterly an eagle. In later years she received other names from different owners before a certain Alexander Baron sold her in Mauritius, in 1857, to Captain Spence of the guano company, De Pass and Spence, who renamed her the *Eagle*. Four years later she was wrecked. In those days Sandwich was a harbour for ocean-going ships, and bird guano was mined from islands in the bay. Alone on the dunes near the *Eagle*, I found it all hard to imagine. I only hoped that some of those early mariners and miners had been able to appreciate the beauty of Sandwich, as I was doing now.

Historical accounts by travellers of those days talk of elephant, rhino and lion in the southern riverbeds, such as the Swakop and Kuiseb, but today these animals are only seen on the northern coast in the area now encompassed by the Skeleton Coast National Park. This is more of a conservation area than a park, in that only small parts of it are open to visitors at certain times of the year. Close to the mouth of the Hoanib, on the Kaokoland coast, is the isolated outpost of Möwe Bay, which I visited in April 1989. This is where the Hoanib elephant come down into the dunes to drink at special water-holes, and lion are also seen here on occasions. Near Torra Bay in 1985, I remember finding lion tracks leading down to the beach. They were so fresh that we followed them until common sense prevailed. We were on foot, and the tawny form of a lion might have been difficult to see in this sandy landscape. The lion come west along the riverbeds and feed on dead fish, seals and occasionally the carcasses of whales.

ABOVE: *'As I skirted the dunes, a sand shark swam by only feet away'*
OPPOSITE: *Small colonies of jackass penguins live on the diamond coast*
BELOW: *Large jelly fish, washed up on the coast in a storm*

At the private invitation of the Nature Conservator, Rod Braby, and his wife, Sigi, I had come to Möwe to join their trip north to the Cunene River mouth, the Angolan border. Our plan was to accomplish the two-hundred-mile journey in convoy. We had two vehicles (my Landcruiser and Rod's Nissan), armed with fuel and provisions for several days, a rubber dinghy and an outboard motor. Thus equipped we headed north on the first leg to Rocky Point. From there, if all went well, we would be able to take advantage of the low tide and drive the whole way on the beach. The inland route was much longer, though safer, but would mean having to camp somewhere along the route. The problem with beach driving, as I had already experienced, was the danger of getting stuck, and the risk of losing a vehicle as the tide came in, but I was all for taking the more direct beach route and that decided it. It was a dazzling day, after the usual misty start, and I followed Rod, leaving a long gap between his vehicle and mine. The skill in this type of driving is to keep as close as possible to the water's edge, but to avoid getting caught by incoming tongues of surf. In the early afternoon I had a near miss. The surface of the beach was gently undulating, and I failed to see

Jackass penguins on parade, an endangered species on this coast

ABOVE, BELOW AND FOLLOWING PAGES: *Fur seals on the Namib coast at Wolf Bay and Baker's Bay*

one of these tongues as it shot in up a little gully. Coming over the rise, I was on it without warning and the wave burst over the front of my vehicle. The engine stopped. Steam rose in clouds as I dried the plugs and distributor, and prayed that Rod would come back. He was now well ahead, out of sight over the horizon. Despite several attempts I could not restart her. Already the wheels were beginning to sink into the sand as the surf swirled around. But then I saw him returning, and I was incredibly relieved. I could not afford to lose my vehicle – there are degrees of drama but that would have been going too far. We attached a cable and Rod successfully winched me to a higher level, away from the surf. My starter-motor was not working, probably full of sand, but with the help of a tow the engine started and we were on our way.

The hinterland of this northern stretch of coastline is different from the southern hinterland, mainly due to its varied, yet subtle colouring, wide horizons and ever-changing light. This is a land of gravel plains, particularly rich in micro life such as scorpions, geckos and chameleons. The plains, often carpeted in lichens, are known as 'lichen fields', where colours become enriched in the evening and early morning light. Added to this is the fog, which enhances the subtle variety of shades and colours. As it is forming it dilutes the sunlight and, breaking up, allows pools and patches of sunlight to fall on the desert below. Behind the gravel plains, only five miles distant, is the northern dune sea which stretches from Torra Bay to the Cunene. It then regroups on the Angola side and sweeps north to the Curoca River. From the coast the dunes appear to float on mirage-lakes, with distant, disembodied mountains beyond. A rare shower of rain in this desolate landscape brings succulents into flower that have been dormant for years.

This part of the Namib can be as bleak and inhospitable as it can at other times be beautiful. In the mid-1800s the British explorer, Charles John Andersson, described his impressions like this:

Ghost crabs at the mouth of the Cunene River

> When a heavy sea-fog rests on these uncouth and rugged surfaces – and it does so very often – a place fitter to represent the infernal regions could scarcely in searching the world round, be found. A shudder, almost mounting to fear, came over me when its frightful desolation first suddenly broke upon my view. 'Death', I exclaimed, 'would be preferable to banishment to such a country.'

Between Rocky Point and the Cunene we passed several wrecks and relics, the first being part of the hull of a Japanese wreck, the *Kia Maru*. Soon afterwards we passed the few remains of the *Dunedin Star* (see Chapter Seven), and just before sunset reached the Cunene River, setting up camp in the shelter of some reeds not far from the dunes. As in the case of the Kuiseb in the central Namib, the Cunene forms a barrier to the dunes' northern progress. The main dune sea stops here, falling precipitously into the river. To the north are rock plains and mountains, with dunes forming again in Angola. Leaving the protection of its valley, the river winds across the flat wind-blown plain, broadening into an estuary with several channels, which branch out through thick reed beds towards the mouth itself. Because the flow of the river cannot normally match the relentless pressure of the ocean currents, a sand-bar has blocked off most of the mouth, forming a sheltered area for migrant birds and crocodiles.

During our time on the Cunene, we made several trips up the river, going as far as the first set of 'serious' rapids. We passed the ghostly remains of the little settlement, Foz do Cunene, abandoned by the Portuguese many years ago. The settlement was rumoured to have been used by the Portuguese as a penal colony and, if true, there would certainly have been no danger of the convicts escaping. I was tempted to explore the deserted buildings but was warned that they could be mined. Instead we explored the islands on the river and estuary, seeing springbok, oryx and

Egrets huddled on a beach north of Angra Fria

plenty of elephant tracks, including a trail of droppings leading right over one of the highest dunes. Crocodiles were everywhere, slipping quietly off sandbanks as we approached. On one occasion, a huge one came straight for the boat and we only just got away in time.

We also took the boat towards the river mouth, getting stuck repeatedly on hidden sandbanks. The water was murky and choppy, which made it impossible to see where the sandbanks were. Time and again both Rod and I were forced to get out in shallow water to push the dinghy off these banks, despite the ever present threat of the crocodiles. Once, we were both pushing hard when Rod gave a yell and leapt into the boat. Being also tense about the situation, I followed suit simultaneously. Together we lay in a nervous heap on the bottom of the boat. It seemed that Rod had stood on a crocodile, which writhed under his feet, but fortunately did not grab him. We had now lost our enthusiasm for getting out of the boat. The only other way of casting off, though less effective, was to try pushing the boat off the sandbank with our paddles. This method seemed to be slowly working, but suddenly the boat came free and I found myself pulled overboard by my

paddle, which was firmly embedded in the sand. I was afraid of losing it, as without an oar we might not have been able to get home. Never have I swum so fast, or climbed back into a boat so speedily, clutching my paddle!

That evening we had a good laugh, re-enacting the whole drama, while Sigi treated the deep cut I had suffered when scrambling into the boat. The whisky tasted good that night, and we exchanged many tall stories round the fire. The stars shone brilliantly in the night sky and the noise of frogs mingled with the distant rumble of the surf, giving us a feeling of infinite remoteness.

FOLLOWING PAGES 116–17: *Rocks sculpted and polished by millennia of riverine erosion, on the banks of the Cunene in western Kaokoland*

FOLLOWING PAGES 118–19: *Fog over the Cunene estuary at dawn*

BELOW: *Desert lion feeding on the carcass of a beached whale on the northern Skeleton Coast*

CHAPTER FOUR

The First Footprints

In May 1989 I travelled north to the Angola border with Chris Eyre and Jason. Chris wanted to know if there were any Himba people living around the Baynes Mountains, following the long guerrilla war between SWAPO and the South Africa forces, which had just ended. The cease-fire was still in its infancy and the 'road' up the eastern side of the Baynes had only just been 'swept' for land-mines. In all probability we were the first non-military vehicle to enter the area for nearly twenty years. I well remember trying in 1981 to organize a helicopter to take me to the Baynes, but no one was prepared to go. 'Too dangerous,' they said. At that time the Baynes represented the ultimate wilderness for me. I would have given anything to get there and now, after all these years, the trip had become a reality. I only hoped that all the land-mines had been removed.

The origin of South Africa's involvement in Namibia goes back to the end of the First World War. Under the terms of the 1918 Treaty of Versailles, Germany was stripped of her colonies, one of which was 'South West Africa' (Deutsche Sudwestafrica). The obvious country to administer this huge wilderness was neighbouring South Africa, still part of the British Empire. Under the terms of a special League of Nations mandate (the League was the precursor of the UN), the then Union of South Africa was entrusted with the administration of South West Africa as an integral part of South Africa, and with leading it to independence as soon as possible.

In 1973, frustrated by South Africa's apparent refusal to give up South West Africa, the United Nations recognized SWAPO as the sole legitimate representative of the Namibian people. From then on money poured into the SWAPO coffers, not only from the United Nations, but from anti-apartheid groups, churches and even governments. Although this money was intended to finance bursaries and scholarships, it was, in practice, used to fund freedom fighters operating out of Angola. For years the SWAPO guerrillas pursued a hit-and-run strategy, planting mines in roads like these, and then hot-footing it back to Angola. One of the first tasks of the United Nations peacekeeping force, which came to Namibia to supervise peaceful elections, was to help remove these mines. The 1989 elections have shown SWAPO to be the dominant political group in Namibia, but not the sole legitimate representative.

Chris explained that, traditionally, this part of Kaokoland formed the eastern sector of Himba territory: it stretches north into Angola, south to the Hoanib, and west into the desert. The Himba are a nomadic offshoot of the Herero people who, according to anthropologists, migrated south from Eastern Africa about three hundred years ago. Herero legend has it that their people came forth at the time of creation from the bowl of a wild fig tree, the only tree in Hereroland that gives shade, and the first man to be born was Mukuru which means the 'ancient one', later synonymous with God. However, they also say that in earlier times they were known as the 'Reed People' because they had originally come from the land of the reeds, perhaps a reference to the lake region of East Africa. During the last century they moved south into present-day Namibia, one group settling in the central highland region, where they came into contact with the first missionaries, from whom the Herero women adopted their colourful Victorian style of dress. The other group,

OPPOSITE: *Himba widow wearing her 'Ekori', a cow-hide head-dress with large ears, fashioned from an ox's cheek or forehead. The head-dress is normally worn on ceremonial occasions, but in this case she is wearing it in mourning for her deceased husband*

later to be known as Himbas, settled in the arid areas of Kaokoland – as it is now known. Out of contact with the white man, they have successfully preserved their traditional lifestyle to this day.

On our second day, we came across a small Himba village near the road. A group of four or five Himbas, dressed traditionally in skins, and one Herero man in western clothes, looked at us in great surprise as we drove up. White visitors were obviously a rarity here. Chris talked to the Herero and discovered that he was a trader spending a few days in the area, having come on foot over the mountains.

'Do you think we will meet any SWAPO guerrillas?' Chris asked.

The Herero replied that there were a few of them around but, 'You will be very unlucky if you meet one!'

He went on to tell us that very few Himbas were currently living in the area because of the war, but he couldn't tell us what we would find further north. He himself had not ventured that far.

At that stage a Himba woman came up, wearing a remarkable cow-hide head-dress which appeared to incorporate the animal's ears. She was covered with red ochre. Chris enquired on my behalf about the significance of her head-dress. He was told that it showed she was in mourning for her husband, who had died two months previously. Apparently widows remain in mourning for up to a year after the death of their menfolk, during which time they wear the head-dress, known as the Ekori, only when they feel like it. They may also wear it for other ceremonies, if they wish.

That night we camped in a sand river lined with huge fig trees and acacias. While I made a fire Chris poured us both a drink and we sat in companionable silence, savouring the cool of the evening after hours of heat and dust. Suddenly we saw a shadow, and a Himba man emerged from the gloom and stood by the fire in his rawhide apron. Chris greeted him in his own language ('Peri nawa,' which means 'Is it good?') and he returned the greeting. We gave him some tobacco, a few crisps and a small tot of rum and he vanished into the darkness looking happy.

Our own food tasted very good and neither of us spoke for a while. In the distance we heard sounds which might be coming from the nearby Himba village, mingled with the noise of crickets, nightjars, plovers and a scops owl. After discussing the state of the world, and especially of Namibia, we laid our bedrolls out by the fire. Chris was snoring within minutes, but I lay awake for a while gazing up at the stars through the tracery of branches, conscious of the reflected glow of embers on the tree. These were special times to remember.

At three in the morning I woke to see Chris climbing noisily out of his sleeping-bag under a starlit sky. Once on his feet he said in bell-like tones, audible from miles away in the stillness of the night, 'Are you awake, David?'

To which I replied, 'No!'

He then asked, 'Any idea what the time is, David? Is it nearly dawn?'

I replied, 'No! It's three o'clock in the morning, Chris, and for God's sake go back to sleep.'

He seemed surprised, and after lighting up a pipe, which he took a long time finding, he climbed back into his bag with a deep sigh.

I woke again at dawn to see thorn trees etched against an orange horizon. I rekindled the fire and put some water on to boil, while we began to pack up camp. It was a beautiful clear morning with a few wisps of cloud catching the first sunlight. Chris and I argued about the food trunk. The jam jar had broken the day before when we hit a big bump, and the jam was over everything – an awful mess. Chris wanted to leave it all until we reached the Cunene River. I thought it might be an idea to clean it up before we broke camp – it was good to be on safari again with Chris!

We continued through a broad mopane-bushed valley, flanked by the seven-thousand-foot

Baynes massif. On the way we passed the burnt-out shell of a vehicle that had hit a land-mine, a sobering reminder of the war. Judging from its condition, no one could have survived. I wondered who the driver had been and when it had happened. Chris explained how even the South African army was scared of this road. 'At one time as many as six land-mines were lifted from a four-mile stretch,' he said. For the rest of the journey to the river I nervously scanned the track ahead for places where the surface might have been 'disturbed'! At all costs we would have to stick to the main track and not deviate onto any minor ones that might not have been swept.

When we finally arrived at the river, I was quite unprepared for what I found. Chris had mentioned that we would pass by the Epupa Falls, but for some reason I had not expected anything so dramatic. The palm-fringed river was broad here, perhaps a quarter of a mile wide, with several islands on which statuesque baobabs grew. The silvery surface of the river reflected the brilliant sunlight, and spray hung continuously in the air, adding a touch of drama to the scene. All around us were bare red mountains, their contrast turning the valley into a lush oasis. As we pulled in under the palms and switched off the engine, I heard the thunder of the falls, as yet unseen. In comparison to other stretches of the river, here the Cunene really looks like a major river that has flowed for a thousand miles from its source in the Angolan highlands. Further downstream I was

PREVIOUS PAGES: *The nomadic Himba live at the edge of a vast wilderness, their territory extending on both sides of the Cunene River, the frontier between Angola and Namibia. To the right are Namibia's Hartmann mountains*

FOLLOWING PAGES: *In the course of our search for Himba people near the Baynes mountains we camped at the Epupa Falls, a magic place where baobabs stood incongruously at the edge of cataracts, like mythical characters from another world*

BELOW: *The Otjihipu range dwarfs a long-deserted Himba village in the Marienfluss*

ABOVE: *Herero village in northern Kaokoland abandoned during the SWAPO/South African war*

able to see how it splits into at least ten different cataracts, with baobabs standing incongruously at the edge of cliffs like mythical characters from a vanished world. In one place, a cataract was split by a boulder dividing the waters into two falls. Perched on the boulder was a baobab, her prehensile roots clinging talon-like to the nooks and crannies, a weathered old matriarch.

Before sunset we followed a game track up the mountain overlooking the falls. The setting was an amphitheatre of bare, gold-red mountains through which the broad river flowed, its green banks fringed with trees. Above the falls were islands with dense clusters of palms, and baobabs on the rocky outcrops amid the cataracts. Rainbows hung over the falls like jewelled sabres, guiding me to some fabulous treasure chest at the bottom of a huge pot of gold. I felt totally absorbed by this landscape, which seemed to bridge the gap between fairytale and earthly reality. The beauty and the fantasy combined to weave a tapestry of magical shapes and impressions.

Later, we walked along the river through the deepening evening shadows, the palm trees silhouetted against an orange and azure sky. Fiery puffs of cloud sailed past, transient images mirrored on the dark silky surface of the river. Earlier we had seen some cattle in the distance: evidently there *were* a few Himbas tucked away in these mountains, who were probably wary of strangers. However, we saw no people, and no recent footprints in the sand.

After supper that evening we laid our bedrolls out by the fire and as I was about to climb into mine, Chris muttered about the dangers of sleeping too close to the river, something about crocodiles. I repositioned my bedroll, putting him between me and the river. I would have said something about the roar of the falls being such that we would never have heard freedom fighters, lions or crocodiles until it was much too late, but by this time Chris was already snoring.

The next day Chris was keen to take a side-track we had passed the previous day, which led west downstream between the river and the Baynes Mountains. On his map it looked as though it might go all the way through to a valley leading between the Baynes and Otjihipu Mountains, where we could pick up another track taking us south. The Otjihipus are a wild, almost impregnable range, which few outsiders have penetrated. My only concern was a half-centimetre gap in the dotted line that indicated the 'road', and I pointed this out to Chris.

'Maybe,' he said, 'but I'm sure it goes through. Why would it just stop like that – it must go through. In any case you'll get a good view of the river and I want to see if there are any Himba there – we might even see some black-faced impala.' (These are one of Africa's most endangered animals.) I was thinking of land-mines again, but since I had noticed the tyre tracks of an armoured car in the sand leading off at yesterday's turning, I decided not to make a fuss. It had obviously been swept. After all Chris knew what he was doing.

Turning off as planned, we drove over a pass into a separate valley leading down to the river again. We stopped at one or two springs – vivid splashes of green in an otherwise barren red landscape – and while Chris scouted round for black-faced impala tracks, I climbed up to look at a desert succulent, a 'poison-bush', covered in beautiful pink flowers, almost like cherry blossom.

Skirting the north-eastern slopes of the Baynes we passed several old Himba huts, probably abandoned in the 1960s. There were no footprints visible in the dust or sand, not even old ones. However, at the bottom of a 'lugga' (dry riverbed), Chris found some fresh black-faced impala tracks. He was very excited.

'You see how long and slender the prints are, and how much bigger they are than an ordinary impala? They are probably drinking at those springs up the valley,' he said, pointing towards the Baynes. 'That's what I'd expect them to do. People told me they were extinct here, shot out by guerrillas, but I always thought that unlikely. The war has obviously kept people out of this area. That's why the impala have survived.'

He went on to tell me that in 1979 the South African army had bowed to local pressure and armed some of the Himba and Herero tribesmen in Kaokoland so that they could protect themselves against SWAPO insurgents. This, coupled with illegal hunting by white army officers, had inevitably led to the decimation of the game. The rifles had never been used against SWAPO.

I asked Chris if we were getting near the Cunene again yet, and he said it was just over the next rise. I looked down at the road and saw that there were no tyre tracks at all: the surface was quite untouched. I pointed this out and Chris said, 'No, the army haven't been this far. I don't think anyone has been along here for years.'

I was now forced to ask about land-mines. 'If neither the army nor the UN (United Nations) have been here, this road hasn't been swept for mines, has it?'

'No, David, it hasn't,' he said, giving me a big grin, 'but don't worry, we'll be all right – we'll just go a little further and see where this track comes out. We needn't go the whole way.'

'You're crazy,' I replied. 'Why take a chance?'

But Chris was unmoved, determined to press on. I even went as far as to suggest that if he wanted to continue he could leave me in the shade of a bush and I would wait for him to come back, but he said he might not return this way so I had to come with him. I was left wondering if he really did have some information which persuaded him that it was safe, or some knowledge he was not divulging so as to see me squirm in my seat with anxiety, or whether he was indeed crazy, as I suspected. I told him of the time, three years before, when flying doctor Mike Wood and I helped evacuate the victims of a land-mine explosion in the Southern Sudan. On that occasion a Landcruiser like ours was blown twenty feet into the air, and a Thames Television producer, Alan Stewart, was killed. I can still see us all standing round the tarpaulin that covered his body, the surviving members of his team numbed with shock, some of them in tears.

'I don't want to go through that again, Chris,' I said.

To which he replied, 'Don't worry, you won't have to because you won't be here.'

Another big grin and I knew he was crazy. What can you do with a man like that?

We passed another long-deserted Himba village with the remains of five tiny huts. There was no sign of a living soul within a hundred miles. Meanwhile the track had been deteriorating and I often had to walk beside the vehicle, heaving rocks out of the way or filling in ruts with smaller stones. The heat was terrific and I felt myself wilting. We scrambled up slopes covered in red boulders, skidding and sliding from side to side, engine screaming. Epic stuff, indeed a little too epic, and it was not getting easier. Had it been my vehicle I would have already said 'enough', yet Chris was used to these conditions and did not bat an eyelid. He just wanted to see if we could get through to the Otjihipus on this road, he said.

Had the journey been more relaxing I might have been more appreciative of the spectacular scenery through which we were travelling. On our left, for instance, the Baynes towered thousands of feet above us while the ground fell steeply to the river on our right. From time to time we caught glimpses of its green and white waters in the gorges below. Immediately opposite, to the north of the river, the Serra Techomalinde range dominated the horizon, an Angolan massif of similar proportions to the Baynes. Meanwhile our track was becoming even more exciting. Coming over a ridge, we plunged six hundred feet into yet another valley, the downward path resembling a watercourse. Often it looked impassable, but by filling in a trench gouged out by past storm waters, and by painstakingly pushing boulders a few inches this way and a few inches that, we managed to get through. What was now worrying me was how on earth we would ever get *back* if it transpired that we could not get through on this road. What if our way was blocked by a washaway, or a landslide? Chris's mind was obviously in the same gear: 'I hope to God we don't have to come back this way – I'm not so sure we'd make it.'

We had reached the bottom of a riverbed leading into the Cunene, and could see the track continuing up the other side, but the river had obviously come down in spate since this track was last used. Our way was blocked by boulders and gullies, so Chris battled along the riverbed while I walked on looking for a point where we could cross. Eventually we managed to find a way, but when trying to climb out of the valley up a very steep incline the wheels just skidded and spun, churning up all the loose stones, digging in rather than making any progress. Again and again Chris reversed and charged the slope, but each time we stuck in the same place

'Why not use the winch?' I suggested. 'It ought to reach that tree up there.'

'Maybe, but we may pull the tree out. This vehicle weighs three tons and the roots of these trees aren't very deep. Let's have one more go before we try it.'

He tried again and, unbelievably, he succeeded. Somehow, inch by inch, the Landcruiser pulled itself up the hill. One wheel would hold while the other three spun. When that wheel began to spin another one would miraculously take over. Meanwhile the vehicle thrashed around like a hooked salmon on the loose surface. If one was going to go on a trip like this, Chris was definitely the man to go with – a brilliant bush driver and an excellent mechanic – and however tough the going got he always had a wicked sideways grin. 'Getting anxious?' he would ask, digging me in the ribs with an elbow, and I had to laugh, and hope that my guardian angel was on duty!

By this time the half-centimetre gap on our map was again nagging me. I also wondered who on earth would have tried to build a road through country like this. It must have taken courage, determination and not a little madness – or did they give up? Was that the explanation for the gap? This was a marathon just going one way, but to have to return as well . . .

'We'll know for certain whether we can get through when we get to that next valley,' said Chris. 'I once came that far approaching from the other side, so I know that there's a track there. We must just get through this next bit – then we can break and have a drink of water.'

It was three o'clock, and we had been following this route for six hours, virtually non-stop. I was thirsty and exhausted from the heat. What I would have given for a cool drink in the shade of a nice tree, but there were no trees here, so we pressed on. The track had become rougher.

'If I'm not mistaken, they built this "road" in 1959,' said Chris, 'and my guess is that very few people, if any, have used it since and certainly not during the last twenty years.'

As he said this, we descended into a shallow ravine and saw a horribly steep, eroded pitch ascending the other side.

'Oh, my God,' said Chris. 'I don't like the look of that. We're definitely going to have to use the winch here.'

Fortunately there was a sturdy little tree at the top of the slope, so I pulled the cable from the winch-drum and hauled it up the bank, sweating profusely. I secured it round the base of the tree, but then became aware that the road deteriorated even more from there on. In fact it was hard to see

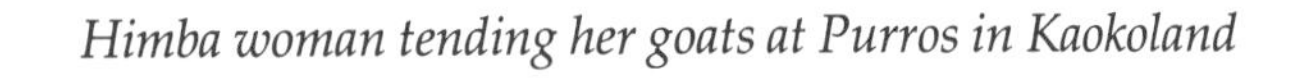
Himba woman tending her goats at Purros in Kaokoland

which way it went. I walked on a bit, following the obvious direction, and to my relief found a section that had clearly been flattened, lined with small stones in an orderly way. I shouted the good news to Chris, who had been similarly depressed. His face lit up, but the euphoria was short lived. The track ended again. We scouted around.

'There's no more road, Chris,' I said. 'I'm afraid this is the end.'

'I don't believe it,' he replied. 'It can't just end, we're nearly there.'

It did seem extraordinary. We could actually see the other track to which Chris had referred – it led in from the Otjihipu side on a ridge a quarter of a mile ahead. It seemed inconceivable that anyone would go to all the effort of building a track through country like this, and then fail to connect up the last half mile. Perhaps they ran out of money, or maybe their labourers went on strike because of man-eating lions, as they once did in Tsavo, Kenya, at the beginning of this century. Clearly there was some reason, and looking at the great ravine that lay between us and the ridge ahead, we knew we were defeated. We would never get a vehicle through there – indeed that itself might have been why they gave up. Whatever the reason, we would have to go all the way back. The map had been right all along: here was the missing half centimetre, in front of our eyes – a 'no through road'.

Chris lit his pipe, frowning. 'Well, if we've got to go back, I suppose we'd better get going.'

My memory of the return trip is a blur of heat and exhaustion, scrambling inch by inch up the rock-strewn slopes, slipping back and trying again. I was mainly on foot, heaving boulders out of the way, pulling stones from beneath the vehicle, carrying flat ones to lay under the wheels, filling in trenches, often blinded by my own perspiration. My friends who think that my life consists of glamorous *Out-of-Africa*-style safaris should have seen me. Sadly there was no other photographer on hand to record these labours.

Although we had failed to get through, we had gone a long way and had achieved two objectives. First, we now knew that the black-faced impala was not extinct in the Baynes. We had found evidence of them which was very encouraging. Second, there were definitely no Himbas living here and there had obviously been none in the area for a very long time. They would have been vulnerable, sitting right on the Angola border, and had sensibly evacuated these slopes in favour of safer pastures, perhaps during the 1970s, maybe even earlier. High up in the Baynes far above our ill-fated route, there might have been a few Tjimbas hidden away in lost valleys. The Tjimbas are relatives of the Himbas and Hereros but, like the Bushmen, do not keep livestock and live by hunting and gathering. It is possible that some of them are still using stone tools.

A few days after our Baynes adventure, Chris and I successfully reached the Otjihipu Mountains using another circuitous route from the south. This time we drove north up the Marienfluss, a huge, wild valley that leads up to the Cunene between the Otjihipu and Hartmann ranges. Here we hoped to see some Himbas and possibly to find some Tjimbas in the secret valleys of the Otjihipus. In 1988 I had flown low over the Otjihipus with Chris and had spotted a narrow valley leading into the range up which we reckoned we could take a vehicle. Our plan now was to find this riverbed, and to follow the gorge into this impregnable mountain fortress.

Some months previously it had rained and the Marienfluss was looking beautiful, carpeted in

PREVIOUS PAGES: *Traditionally Himba territory, the Marienfluss lies between the Hartmann and Otjihipu mountains, in northern Kaokoland. A shepherd's tree,* Boscia albitrunca, *clings to a rocky outcrop*

OPPOSITE: *Himba lives revolve round their livestock, their cattle in particular. Cattle are still the main indication of wealth and status in their society*

long, golden grass, a hazard for Landcruiser radiators! Seen thus it looked more like a prairie than a desert, and I found it hard to reconcile this image with an aerial photo I had seen of mountain zebra galloping across a red sandy valley without a blade of grass or other vegetation. Dominating the middle of the valley was the island mountain, Ondao, sacred to the Himba people. Named after a special tuba (root) found near the Cunene, which they hang around their necks or ankles in place of beads, this mountain is the burial place of their ancestors. A few years ago the son of the Himba Headman Vetamuna was killed by SWAPO guerrillas, leaving him broken-hearted. Following the old custom, he went down to Ondao in the Marienfluss to the grave of his great-grandfather, to see which way the war was going. At the grave he sacrificed a black sheep with a white spot, and spent time communing with the ancestral spirits.

Opposite Ondao we picked up the sand river we were looking for and followed it up towards the Otjihipus, which now dominated the eastern horizon. As we came closer to the mountains, the riverbed seemed to disappear at the base of the cliffs. There was no sign of any valley, yet it had to come from somewhere. Only at the last minute did the gorge reveal itself, a deep cleft leading into the massif with huge cliffs rising hundreds of feet on either side. Entering the gorge, we once again found ourselves battling in four-wheel drive over loose stones in the riverbed. Frequently our route was blocked by rocky banks and gullies and we were forced to try different ways. Again there were boulders which had to be moved, and routes that had first to be reconnoitred on foot. From the air it had all looked so easy, but now we half expected to find our passage irretrievably blocked round every corner. It was late afternoon so the gorge was largely in shade, but shafts of sunlight were poking through like spotlights, revealing wild chestnuts growing on the cliffs far above us: a beautiful, peaceful place. Even in the shade it was hot.

To his credit Chris succeeded in fighting his way nearly six miles into the heart of the mountains, until finally we were barred by a dry waterfall. We could go no further. On our way we had picked up a Himba who wanted a lift back to his village. (The Himbas walk huge distances between villages, resting in the shade of trees when the sun gets too hot.) He now told us of a rock pool upstream, above the 'waterfall'. Years ago he had come here as a child and remembered the pool. Chris and I were desperate from heat and thirst so we eagerly followed him, thinking that the pool would be just round the corner. It turned out to be a half hour's hard walking and scrambling, yet worth the effort once we were there. The water was beautifully clear and sweet, in a cleft so narrow that the sunlight probably never reached it. On the sand nearby we found fresh tracks of mountain zebra, but no human spoor.

When we got back to our vehicle it was nearly dark, and we gathered firewood and found flat places on the rocks for our bedrolls. The stones in the river bed were crawling with corn crickets, huge red, green and purple animals with thick bodies and three-inch legs. They move very slowly and look like something out of a horror film. They also spend most of their time eating each other.

As we ate our supper in tired silence round the fire, the moon came out from behind a ridge above, flooding the gorge in a silvery light. Huge crags stood silhouetted against the night sky, and the boughs of an overhanging ana tree reflected the flickering firelight. Only the clear, fluting call of a spotted eagle owl and the distant whistle of a nightjar broke the stillness. Our Himba friend was already asleep and Chris and I turned in early, too. I could see from the glow in his direction that he was enjoying a last pipe as he lay in his sack, watching the stars.

Despite the bumpy ground I was asleep in no time, but woke in the night to see a large corn cricket silhouetted in the moonlight, climbing over the pillow towards me, only inches from my face. I nearly screamed, it was such a horrible sight. After removing this ugly predator I noticed several other monsters lit up on the legs and arms of my camping chair, which they had somehow scaled despite the aluminium surface. Oviously they had sticky feet, and I did not fancy the idea of those feet on my face. I noticed how slowly and deliberately they moved, waving their legs like moon-worshippers, dancing to a secret rhythm. Meanwhile unseen bats whirred round me emitting their electronic clicks, and the fire gave a final dying hiss.

When I woke at first light the eagle owls were calling close by in the early morning stillness and I lay there savouring the wildness of the place. Thanks to Chris I had achieved a long-term ambition to penetrate these mountains. It had been even more difficult than I had expected, but worthwhile. To my great frustration, however, there was no more time to explore, so we drove back to the Marienfluss the way we had come.

Near the entrance of the gorge was another deserted Himba village which Chris and I had seen from the air and imagined to be occupied. We found no sign of recent habitation, though. Instead we headed south along the Marienfluss to Okatapati, where our Himba passenger lived. As I had hoped, Okatapati was an unspoilt village. No roads led there – it was just a question of driving over the sandy (now grassy) plains, looking out for hidden pig holes (dug by warthogs, which live down them). Chris had been there before so the people knew him, but this time he had no interpreter and communication was therefore difficult. His only word seemed to be 'peri nawa', which according to him passed for 'hello', 'good', 'nice', 'OK' and 'goodbye' as well as 'is it good?'. In places like this people have never seen a camera, and trying to explain that you want to photograph someone can be difficult. They are also unfamiliar with our sign language, and merely looked at me as if I was

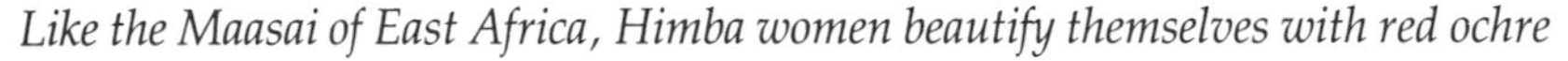

Like the Maasai of East Africa, Himba women beautify themselves with red ochre

ABOVE LEFT: *Himba men are ardent pipe smokers and tobacco chewers. The skewer is for scratching under the turban when the coiffure becomes itchy*

ABOVE RIGHT: *They water their livestock from springs and wells dug in riverbeds*

OPPOSITE: *Himba girl at a desert spring in western Kaokoland*

mad when I started gesticulating. The chief himself seemed to understand, but this did not appear to help. In the end I found that the best solution was to sit in the shade of a bush and watch the Himba world go by. Gradually the villagers became accustomed to my presence and I was able to photograph various activities, like milking goats, fetching water, grinding corn, and women putting on their red ochre make-up.

The children were the least suspicious and the most intrigued by what I was doing. Himba boys wear the traditional leather apron and the metal beaded collar that all the men appear to wear. Their heads are shaven except for a central strip of hair which is plaited into a single pigtail at the back. When they get married they have to wear their hair longer, and keep it all wrapped in a large turban of cloth or softened sheep skin. You often see a skewer behind their ear, which they use to scratch under the turban when their coiffure gets itchy. Himba girls wear their hair in two plaits hanging over the forehead. When they get married they wear their hair lengthened into long thin braids. On the top of their heads is a soft skin headpiece signifying their married status. Their bodies are always adorned with necklaces and belts, and a special white conch pendant that hangs between their bare breasts. These shells are traded through Angola, having originally come all the way from the east coast of Africa, and are usually the women's most treasured possessions. Most striking of all, though, are their spiral copper armlets and iron beaded anklets. Beautiful soft buck skins hang from their hips.

Like East Africa's Maasai, the Himbas' lives revolve around their livestock, their cattle in particular. Cattle are still the main indication of wealth and status in their society, but, as with the Maasai, they do not normally eat them, slaughtering them only for special ceremonies such as weddings, name-givings, circumcisions and funerals. The cattle skins themselves are an important raw material used for mats, blankets, bags and clothing. Himba children are initiated into the mysteries of the cattle culture from an early age. Himba boys are sent out to herd goats and sheep when they are only five or six years old, often sleeping out in the desert for a night or two to protect the animals against predators – a heavy responsibility for a six-year-old. There are few lions left in Kaokoland these days, but there is always the possibility of an occasional pride, and even leopard, which are still common in these mountains. Hyena and snakes can be dangerous and frightening.

The Himbas and Hereros are tobacco chewers and ardent pipe-smokers, mostly the men but also the women, particularly the Herero women. When you have something to discuss with a Himba you sit down in the shade of a tree with him, and the first thing he does is light up his pipe. It is always tactful to wait until it is lit before making any proper conversation. As in other rural areas of Africa, it is also customary to talk first about general issues, such as the lack of rain and the condition of the cattle and goats, before broaching the main topic. The more important or delicate the topic is, the longer the period of introductory small talk. Pipe-smoking is a pleasant way of

OPPOSITE: *The natural beauty and dignity of a Himba woman in Kaokoland*

BELOW: *Himba children with traditional hairstyles, the boy with a central strip of hair, and the girl with her hair in two plaits over the forehead*

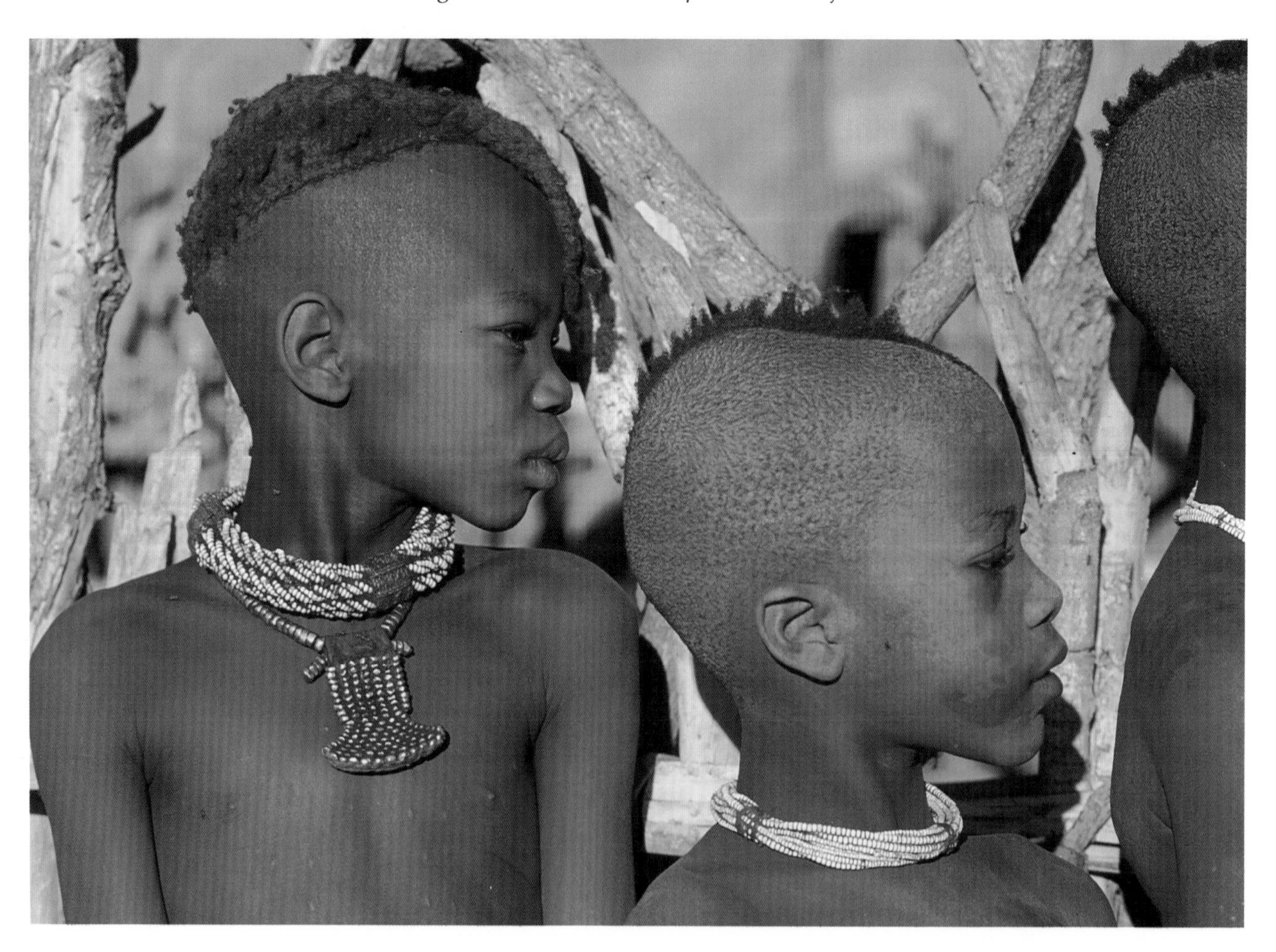

ABOVE: *Himbas normally keep dogs, and occasionally horses*

OPPOSITE ABOVE: *Purros, a Himba settlement in south-western Kaokoland*

OPPOSITE BELOW: *When Himba girls are married they wear their hair lengthened into long thin braids, with a soft buck-skin headpiece on the top of their heads, signifying their married status*

spinning out these preliminaries. My father has always smoked a pipe and he told me years ago how useful it was at big conferences. When people fired awkward questions at him, he could light up his pipe, take a deep pull on it, and then answer the question. Those precious extra seconds were worth their weight in gold, and when his answer finally came, the pipe gave it a certain profundity.

Although the Himbas are the only people still leading a traditional life in the desert in any significant numbers, they are not the original inhabitants of the Namib. The honour of that title must fall to the Bushmen, or San as they are now also known, and perhaps on the ancestors of the Damara, or on the Bergdamara – who 'lived in the mountains'. Bushmen have probably lived in the Namib for thousands of years, and in places you see their vivid rock paintings and engravings which remind you of their rich culture and mythology. Small in stature, like the pygmies of Zaire, the Bushmen were almost certainly the original inhabitants of Southern Africa and, like the pygmies, they were hunter-gatherers. This brought them progressively into conflict with migrant black pastoralists from the north, and latterly white settlers from the south. Unlike these new-comers, they lived in total harmony with their environment. Their herds were wild beasts and their fruit and vegetables whatever nature chose to grow: for tens of thousands of years they lived in Africa's Eden.

In April 1989 I returned to a place called Twyfelfontein, which means 'doubtful spring', in the mountains of central Damaraland. The hillside here is covered in large red boulders, many of which

have been decorated with thousands of beautiful engravings, mostly depicting animals such as eland, rhino, giraffe and lion, painstakingly pecked out of the rock. Twyfelfontein ranks as one of Africa's most important rock art sites, with the Tsodilo Hills in Botswana, and the Sahara's Tassili Plateau. Although I had been there previously, I saw engravings that I had not seen before, notably the 'dancing kudu', a beautiful panel. This one combines animal representations with schematic (abstract) designs, similar to ones which I have photographed at Daberas in the southern Namib, near the Orange River. The latter were white on blue-grey marble slabs. The designs have yet to be deciphered, but some archaeologists believe that they were inspired by dreams. There is still doubt and controversy about their age, partly because very little archaeological work has yet been done at Daberas. Some say that these schematic designs are far older than the animal designs, but most experts I have spoken to maintain that they are more recent. I remember being told at the Tsodilo Hills, where white schematics were mixed with red animal paintings, that the Bushmen, or San, who lived there maintained that the white ones were painted by their ancestors, and the red ones by God. This seems to indicate that the white ones are more recent, but there is no conclusive evidence. The engravings at Daberas may have been made by Hottentots.

In March 1989, in the southern Namib, I found old chips of ostrich eggshell in the Aurus Mountains and surrounding hills, a sure sign of former San (Bushman) habitation. On the same trip, nearer the coast, I also found quantities of stone tools exposed by the shifting sands. There were probably San living in some of these areas until just after World War II. In Luderitz I found that as recently as 1931 a tiny community of San was discovered by the police, living in the Aurus

Mountains. At a remote water-hole they found seventeen men, women and children living off ostrich eggs, roots and honey, and occasional animals that they managed to shoot. The poor San would have been told that they were living 'illegally' in the forbidden diamond area, and would have to move out. In those days no one had any time for the San; they were still thought of as lesser mortals, even vermin, as they still are today in parts of the Kalahari. History does not relate what became of the Aurus clan.

Nearby, I was also told an interesting story by Jan Coetzer, a security officer working for CDM, who had been brought up on a farm near Aus. He remembered that a European prospector was said to have been killed by Bushmen some time in the early 1940s. One of the local farmers, whom he described as being a hard old man and 'very tough on his labour' (though 'he always read the Bible to them on Sunday'), set out to find the culprits. Eventually he succeeded and shot them dead, three little people who may have been the last San of the Namib. In those days it was not a serious crime to shoot a Bushman, particularly if he was suspected of committing some offence. Jan, being young at the time, was not sure where the incident had taken place, but it might have been in the Awasib Mountains, north-west of Aus. In 1986 Chris Eyre and I found three unmarked graves there, with crude headstones, along with fragments of ostrich eggshell, but the graves were of European design. Perhaps the farmer buried them – a last gesture of respect.

In the desert I always camp out under the stars, which for me is one of the greatest experiences that life has to offer. Only occasionally, when lions, hyenas or heavy rainfall threaten, do I sleep in a

OPPOSITE: *Herero women owe their colourful Victorian style of dress to the influence of early European missionaries and their wives*

BELOW: *A Herero woman enjoying a pipe*

OPPOSITE AND ABOVE (detail): *Rock engraving in the diamond area near the Orange River, probably executed by Hottentot (Khoi) people*

PREVIOUS PAGES: *The original inhabitants of the Namib were Bushmen (San hunter-gatherers) who left a record of their lives and dreams on the caves and shelters of their desert world. This ancient engraving, measuring five feet across, is known as the 'dancing kudu'*

tent. Out in the open I lose myself in the desert stillness, and in the myriad stars above. At times I think of the San and their mythology-related universe. Gazing into these brilliant constellations, it is very easy to see how their imagination was fired. They believe, for example, that the stars are great hunters and that if you listen you can hear their hunting cries, 'Tsa, Tsa'. There is certainly an audible quality to the intense silence which I have experienced camping out in the desert, like the distant murmuring of a million celestial voices. When I think of what the San say, and listen hard, I too can hear those hunters of the sky.

The other early inhabitants of this land were the Damara and Bergdamara, whose identity and dignity were swamped by their old masters. They appear in the earliest records and seem to have been servants to the Nama and Hereros, even occasionally to the San. They had an ancient language of their own, but this has been lost in the mists of time. They now speak a Khoi language almost identical to Nama. According to some accounts the Hereros used to call the Bergdamara 'Ovazorotua', or 'black slaves', and unlike their own legend about having come forth at the time of creation from a wild fig tree, they believed that the Bergdamara had less distinguished origins, namely that, together with the goats and baboons, they had come out of a rock which split open.

Although the Bushmen certainly came first, the people most closely associated with the Namib were the Nama, by whom most of the rivers and mountains were named. 'Namib' itself is a Nama name, as are Kuiseb, Ugab, Swakop, Hoanib, Awaseb and Hauchab. The Nama were Hottentots, or Khoi, and said to be descended from the so-called 'Red Nation', who came south from the Kalahari during the eighteenth century and then moved west along the Orange River. The Dutch settlers called them Hottentots, which meant 'stammerers', referring to their 'click' language, which sounded so extraordinary to a European. In recent years the name Hottentot has acquired derogatory connotations and fallen into disfavour. These people shared a common origin with the Kalahari Bushmen, who also speak a click language, but the main difference between them originally was that the Khoi had livestock and the San did not. In addition there were linguistic (different clicks) and other cultural differences, but physically they were very similar, sometimes grouped and referred to by anthropologists as Khoisan. The Nama were livestock herders, and enjoyed augmenting their herds by raiding other tribes, who feared them for their bravery and cunning (particularly after they were joined by the Orlams in the 1800s). The cattle raiding took them to parts of the Namib which they would probably not have visited otherwise, and this accounts for many of the rivers and mountains receiving Nama names.

The Orlams were of mixed Khoi and European descent and migrated north from the Cape during the nineteenth century. The name 'Orlams' meant the 'smart guys', and the Nama and Orlams gradually merged to become one people. The most famous Orlam leader was Jonker Afrikander, who made his base in Windhoek and led a commando of two hundred Nama and Orlams north to raid the Owambo people in the mid-1800s. The Owambo, a large tribe in the north-eastern corner of Namibia, were apparently seriously intimidated, capitulating without a fight, and allowed Jonker to capture huge numbers of cattle. This unfortunately rebounded on Jonker because some of the cattle had a disease which was thereby taken south. The disease, probably rinderpest, spread rapidly and both the new cattle and Jonker's existing stock died, leaving his people with nothing. Jonker himself contracted malaria after the raid, and never fully recovered.

Of the various Nama sub-tribes, one in particular is associated with the Namib – the Topnaars. These people had lived in the desert since long before the Orlam migration and were completely adapted to their harsh environment. They were consequently never numerous, and have now all but disappeared as a group except for two or three small communities, living in the Kuiseb valley in the central Namib. In April 1989 I drove down from Windhoek to meet some of them.

The first place I visited was Homeb, where the Kuiseb runs along the northern edge of the southern dune sea. This area falls within the 'Namib Park', but the authorities have sensibly placed it out of bounds to tourists so that the Topnaars can retain their privacy. It is one of the most interesting parts of the desert, because here the sand-dunes meet the vast gravel plains of the central Namib. Crossing the Kuiseb near Henno Martin's first hideaway, Carp Cliff, I drove over the plains as thunder-clouds massed on the eastern horizon. Vegetation was almost non-existent, yet there was an untouched purity to the plains which was beautiful. I had already sent a message to the Topnaar chief – or 'captain', as the Nama chiefs have always been known – to say that I was coming, and on arrival was met by his father, the former captain, who had recently handed over to his son. I found him standing outside his hut built from river driftwood, a small bearded old man with clear brown eyes. Like his father and his grandfather his name was Khoitjie (pronounced 'Koikie'). He is Eso Khoitjie and his son is Sid Khoitjie. Khoitjie means 'son of Khoi'.

In *Lords of the Last Frontier*, Lawrence Green told a story of how many years ago, when the British ruled Southern Africa, the Topnaar captain traditionally drew an allowance of six pounds for loyal service. When this came up for annual renewal in the Cape parliament it was customary for someone to ask in jest, 'But who is the Topnaar captain?' To which the standard reply was, 'Why, he's the captain of the Topnaars.' In those days, writes Green, stories were passed down of the ceremony in March 1878 when Commander Dyer of the Royal Navy annexed Walvis Bay, formerly Walfisch or Whale Bay, in the name of Queen Victoria.

The Navy realized the strategic importance of the bay on a coast otherwise devoid of natural

A community of Topnaar Nama (Khoi) living by the Kuiseb riverbed

harbours. The only other harbour of any size was Angra Pequeña, Portuguese for 'Little Bay', which was annexed by the Germans six years later. Angra Pequeña was later renamed Lüderitz-bucht (Lüderitz Bay) in honour of the trader Adolf Lüderitz who established a trading station there. North of Walvis Bay is Swakopmund, a resort town built by the Germans. These three are the only proper towns on the entire coastline between the Cunene and Orange Rivers. Walvis Bay is today an important commercial port and the centre of a thriving fishing industry. For the time being it continues to be a South African enclave in Namibian territory. In its defence, South Africa argues that Walvis Bay has never formed part of the territory of Namibia. Even in the German days it was a British enclave in German territory.

I talked to Eso Khoitjie about the coming 'nara' harvest, the big annual event in the Topnaar culture. Naras are melons which grow in the nara fields in the dunes further down the Kuiseb Valley. Each Topnaar family has its own field, and early each year they go down the river to harvest the naras. The sweet-tasting pulp is boiled, and after the seeds have been removed it is poured onto the sand to dry into a pancake which is stored all year. The seeds themselves are mostly sold to dealers in Walvis Bay, and thence exported as a delicacy to the Cape, South Africa. The Topnaars also have a limited number of cattle which are left to graze in the Kuiseb.

On many parts of the Namib coast there are strange circles of pointed stones about eight foot in diameter, the remains of Strandloper huts surrounded by ancient middens of fishbones and clam shells. The Strandlopers were simple people who lived along the Namib coast, surviving on shellfish and seals, whose way of life has become extinct. Originally they were said to be Bushmen who, like others, had been persecuted and were thus secretive people hiding away on remote parts of the coast. Now most anthropologists believe that they were never a distinct ethnic group, even though the first Strandlopers may have been Bushmen. It is thought that most were of Khoi descent, the majority being Topnaars.

There might also have been two different types of Strandloper, the first being seasonal, coming down to the coast (from Sesfontein, in recent times) to harvest the nara melons in the dry river estuaries. This group could even have included Himbas, Hereros and Damara, who resorted to a temporary Strandloper existence during the times of prolonged drought. The second group, who have long since disappeared, would have been those that lived and scavenged permanently up and down the coast, looking for seals and, in particular, whales. These might have included San (Bushmen), and are likely to be the people described by the early Kaokoland explorers, Hartmann (1900) and Elyers (1906), as 'constantly walking up and down the coast in search of whales that come ashore, and you will find their kraals all the way to Khumib (a river between the Cunene and the Hoanib Rivers) and also a long way south to the Hoanib'.

On my last visit to Namibia I was told by several people of two San living at Sesfontein, who had been Strandlopers in their younger days. In Damaraland, Blythe Loutit told me that she had met some former Strandlopers (whom she thought were San) at Sesfontein, who had told her of the days when they used to go down to the Uniab delta and live off fish and nara melons. The last time they were there was in the 1950s. I have since talked to Windhoek anthropologist Wilfried Haacke, who told me that he had met an old Topnaar woman at Sesfontein called Gamkas. She had once lived at Ausas water-hole in the Hoanib dunes with a small Topnaar community, leading a Strandloper existence. As far as he knew she was now dead, the last of the Sesfontein Strandlopers.

In October 1988 I drove up to the Hartmann Valley in Kaokoland, west of the Marienfluss, and found a number of Strandloper hut circles high above the Cunene. I later talked to Chris Eyre about

OPPOSITE: *A Topnaar woman*

Nama prisoners with their German guard during the Hottentot uprisings (WINDHOEK ARCHIVES)

this, and he said that the Himba Headman Vetamuna had told him that the Hartmann circles were made by Himbas. This supports the theory that the name 'Strandloper' really referred to a way of survival practised by most of the Namib people from time to time, during periods of prolonged drought, rather than to a specific tribe or race. Even today rainfall, or the lack of it, dictates the actions, movements and lifestyle of many of the Namib people, but before the days of wind-pumps and boreholes these effects were more dramatic. When the wells ran dry then the Nama and the Himbas went in search of pasture for their stock regardless of tribal boundaries, and of the fighting that might result. Their cattle came first and when these died from disease or were stolen in raids, they became Strandlopers and hunter-gatherers until the next rains came.

Sesfontein is now a mixed community of Hereros, Damara and Khoi people. During the last century the Swartbooi Khoi (Hottentots – one of the Orlam groups from the Cape) joined up with some of the Topnaars and went north to Sesfontein to make a new home and escape from the endless wars with the Hereros. All went well until the Germans arrived in Namibia and raised their imperial flag. In 1898 the Swartboois rebelled against their German overlords, and in consequence were almost annihilated as a people. The Hereros followed suit in 1904, receiving similar punishment at the battle of Waterberg. The survivors of the Swartbooi rebellion had their land confiscated, but were later allowed to settle on a small circular reserve at Sesfontein, which they shared with the Topnaar remnant. The ruined German fort at Sesfontein dates from these days.

The last of the great Nama chiefs, or captains, who for years led the Germans a dance, was Hendrik Witbooi of the Witbooi Khoi. Like the Swartboois, the Witboois were really Orlams from the Cape who had rebelled against the Dutch and migrated north, taking firearms and horses (as well as language and religion) with them. They settled in the more fertile central region of southern Namibia and gradually extended their influence north and north-east. Despite the warlike reputation of his men, Hendrik Witbooi was a literate Christian with a missionary background, and in many senses a gentleman. He had a clear sense of justice and a natural commitment to the principle of self-determination. He would not accept, for instance, that Germany had a right to make him a second-class citizen in his own land.

ABOVE LEFT: *Hendrik Witbooi, the Nama chief, who for years led the Germans a dance operating from his mountain stronghold at Naukluft* (WINDHOEK ARCHIVES)

ABOVE RIGHT: *General von Trotha* (top) *was the strong man sent by the Germans to replace Major Leutwein* (bottom) *who was considered too moderate* (WINDHOEK ARCHIVES)

Germany's involvement in Namibia began in 1883, when Adolf Lüderitz established his trading station at Angra Pequeña, between the Orange River and Walvis Bay. Under the terms of a treaty with the Hottentot Chief Josef Fredricks, signed at Bethanie – a hundred and forty miles inland – he bought a strip of desert adjacent to the coast, where he planned to build a general-purpose factory and a harbour. Here, for a while, he traded European goods for ivory and ostrich feathers with the Khoi who lived in the Namib interior. Generally speaking they were friendly people, but not long after he had landed he sent requests to the German Government for protection, doubtless hoping they would annex the territory and thus make his job easier. These initial requests were, in fact, refused and soon afterwards Adolf Lüderitz went bankrupt. Ironically, his land was purchased by the newly-formed German Colonial Company. In 1884 the German flag was hoisted at Angra Pequeña, to be called Lüderitzland.

Another treaty was drawn up with Fredricks at Bethanie. Under its terms a vast tract of Africa, nearly half the size of the German Reich, was effectively purchased by Germany for a 'song'. South West Africa was formally declared a German Protectorate in January 1884 at a small ceremony in Angra Pequeña. Britain had already annexed Walvis Bay and had been expected to step in after Germany's original refusal to co-operate over protection. Indeed, the British had been approached by several of the local chiefs, seeking protection from the Boers and Germans. But Britain took so long to make up her mind that the German Government took control. To protect German interests and property, the first Schutztruppe ('protection force') was established. Although small at first, this soon became the German Colonial Army in the territory, which browbeat and bludgeoned the local tribes into submission.

All tribal chiefs were required to sign a protection treaty whereby the German Government would defend them against would-be aggressors. Many chiefs signed, although some did not understand that in so doing they were signing away their freedom. Witbooi was prominent amongst the few who did not see the point of such a treaty, and was therefore not willing to sign. He reasoned that he could look after himself and did not need the German Reich to protect him. Having already rebelled against the Dutch in the Cape, he knew all about the white man's devious ways and tried to warn other chiefs against signing treaties with the Germans, but they all gradually fell into line, though not before Witbooi refused to sign.

The Schutztruppe made its first surprise attack on Witbooi at Hoornkrans in the central highlands in 1892; but Witbooi simply withdrew into the Naukluft mountains at the edge of the Namib. Despite the heat and arid conditions the Naukluft range had good water and proved to be an ideal stronghold for him. It took two years for the Germans to flush Witbooi out, yet as he pulled back he managed to negotiate more and more favourable terms of surrender. When he finally succumbed and signed the treaty of friendship and protection, he was allowed to retain both his rifles and his captaincy.

In 1981, nearly a hundred years later, I spent several days in these mountains, exploring the secret valleys and looking at the places where Witbooi made his stands. It was still possible to find old cartridge cases and magazines from that campaign. In one of the valleys I was shown where the Germans had hauled their cannons up into the hills. You could still see where they had made a ramp up the slope and I wondered who had come off best in the ensuing engagement. Nearby was the grave of a German soldier dated 1894. I had also heard of the deep rock pools where Witbooi had watered livestock and warriors, and decided to walk over the top to see one of them.

It took me a long hot day to reach the pool and I shall never forget the blissful relief of diving into that deep, crystal-clear water.

During the time that Witbooi was fighting in the Naukluft, he and the Schutztruppe Commander, Major Leutwein, developed a degree of respect for each other. Letters and notes would pass between them, such as the following from Witbooi, jotted in red pencil on a scrap of paper whilst in full retreat:

> . . . I have received your letter on the run, and note that you are willing to negotiate. I agree to stop shooting, if you keep your men out of the mountains. I shall reply to your letter from the water-hole. Be patient: I am in a dry place without water. It would be best for you to await my reply at Naauwkloof. I am going in that direction now. Send some writing paper, and some tabacco and coffee and tea . . .

After Witbooi surrendered he kept the peace for ten years and even fought alongside the Germans in several uprisings, including the Herero rebellion in 1904. He kept his word to Leutwein, who by this time had become governor of the colony, but Leutwein soon fell into disfavour with his superiors for being too humane and moderate. He was consequently replaced by General von Trotha, whose solutions were genocidal. Witbooi was upset. His peace agreement had been with Leutwein, whom he trusted. The new man was arrogant and autocratic. The time had come for the Red Nation (both Orlams and Nama) to reclaim its sovereignty and, at the age of eighty, Hendrik Witbooi called on the other captains to join him in this crusade against the Germans. Several did, and soon Witbooi's guerrilla army numbered nearly two thousand.

This time the fighting took place over large parts of southern Namibia and soon developed into a protracted guerrilla war. During an eighteen-month period there were at least two hundred small battles and the more the fighting dragged on, the more discredited von Trotha became. German morale was low and Witbooi was again invited to surrender. His reply to von Trotha read as follows: 'Peace would be death to me and to my nation. For I know there is no domicile for me under you.'

In October 1905, not long after writing this, Witbooi was fatally wounded while taking part in a raid on a German supply column. He was hit in the thigh and later died from loss of blood. His last words were, 'It is over. I am done for. Now the children can rest.' The uprising collapsed and Witbooi's men rode in to surrender their weapons, proud and erect in their saddles. Von Trotha was overjoyed, but Witbooi's old sparring partner, Leutwein, wrote a widely publicized obituary, of which the following is an extract:

> The name of the little captain will . . . remain engraved upon the history of South West Africa for ever. His stubborn resistance against the mighty German Empire at the head of a small warlike band. . . . Fully understanding the superior culture of the whites, yet by no means always in love with those who purveyed it – a born leader and ruler: this was Witbooi, who would undoubtedly have become an immortal in world history had not the fates ordained him to be born to an insignificant African throne. He was the last national hero of a race doomed to destruction.

FOLLOWING PAGES: *One of the limestone pools in the Naukluft mountains where Witbooi was based during his long struggle against the Germans*

BELOW: *This old hutcircle may have been made by Khoi people (Hottentots)*

CHAPTER FIVE

Blood, Sweat and Horses

Horses were first introduced to this territory long ago by Nama traders who brought them up from the Cape. It was a tough environment for a horse but the Afrikaner nag was a tough breed. There were areas of the desert which horses found hard going, particularly the dunes and heavy sands of the Namib and Kalahari. This prompted the Germans to import large numbers of camels (the camel was not indigenous to southern Africa), which were used by the Schutztruppe with great effect in their wars against the Nama. They were also used for transport and police patrols in the diamond fields near Luderitz.

Young German soldiers with equestrian experience were in demand as Schutztruppe recruits. A good example of such horsemen was the eccentric Baron Hansheinrich von Wolf. There was doubt, it seems, as to whether von Wolf was a real baron or whether he perhaps acquired the title in South West Africa because of his grand life style. In any event, he was a Prussian cavalry officer who volunteered for the Schutztruppe and arrived as a captain in 1904.

It was the time of the great Nama uprising against the Germans led by Hendrik Witbooi. Newly-recruited officers like von Wolf came out expecting to fight against a native rabble that was no match for its Caucasian overlords. Instead they found a highly-mobile, well-armed force who were skilled in the art of guerrilla warfare. After an embarrassingly short time, von Wolf suffered a serious setback when he was forced to retreat and abandon his guns to a superior Hottentot force. Disgraced and humiliated, he had to resign his commission. He returned to Dresden, licking his wounds.

At this low ebb in his life, he had the good fortune to meet Jayta Humphries, whose wealthy stepfather was the American Consul General in Dresden. Jayta made light of his disgrace and seems to have persuaded him to return to South West Africa. Perhaps she realized that only by returning would he be able to heal the wounds of humiliation. On his return, he and Jayta bought themselves a fifty-thousand-acre farm, Duwisib (meaning 'place of the rainbow'), with Jayta's money. The farm was subsequently extended to cover a total of 35,000 acres. Duwisib is situated about two hundred miles south-west of Windhoek at the eastern edge of the Namib.

Here they set about building themselves a real castle, with twenty-two rooms, a cellar and numerous outbuildings. Wilhelm Stander was appointed as architect. Special carpets, furniture and building materials were shipped out from Europe, and Italian stonemasons were employed full-time, along with three carpenters from Denmark, Ireland and Sweden. It took twenty ox-wagons two years to transport all the iron and timber needed across the Namib from Luderitz, a journey of some four hundred miles. The interior walls were decorated with fine horse prints, swords, rifles and animal trophies. The local people must have looked on in wonder at the extraordinary edifice that rose before their eyes. The castle was still very much intact when I visited Duwisib in 1986. The furniture and pictures had only recently been temporarily removed to Windhoek for an exhibition, but otherwise the 'Schloss' had not changed substantially since von Wolf's day. One of the upstairs bedrooms in the tower was decorated with a feminine touch, a beautiful painted ceiling, and must have been a lady's room, perhaps Jayta's.

Legend has it that von Wolf was a great practical joker and popular in his district, Maltahöhe, where he was soon elected to represent it in the Legislative Assembly. There is an old photograph of

OPPOSITE AND FOLLOWING PAGES: *Wild horses whose origins go back to the German colonial days, before World War I. In the diamond area west of Aus, near the Garub spring*

Detachment of camel-mounted Schutztruppe, the German colonial army (WINDHOEK ARCHIVES)

all the Assembly members grouped together, von Wolf being the only person present wearing a hat – a sign of his eccentricity. In 1908 von Wolf heard that diamonds had been discovered near Luderitz, and immediately trekked down across the Namib to stake out some claims. According to one account he is said to have crossed to Meob Bay, north-west of Duwisib, and then travelled south to Luderitz. He became good friends with August Stauch during this period. Stauch was a fellow member of the Legislative Assembly and the man who discovered the first diamonds.

Horses were von Wolf's first love and he soon established a reputation as a breeder. English thoroughbreds and Prussian trakehners were imported from Europe and crossed with Afrikaner mares to produce a hardy strain. His most famous stallions were an Australian horse called Neptune and an Irish one named Crackerjack, who sired many fine horses and won him a number of trophies. As the Schutztruppe expanded its force, more and more horses were needed, and increasingly these came from von Wolf's reputable stables.

Just before the outbreak of war, he and Jayta, and a friend, von Dewitz, left for Europe on a stallion-buying trip. While they were at sea war was declared and the vessel changed course for a South American port, where the passengers were interned. Through contacts, the party was soon released, and they boarded a neutral ship bound for Europe. When the ship put in at Vigo in Sweden the two men pretended to disembark while Jayta remained on board. However, she in fact stowed them away in her cabin and the story goes that the steward was amazed at the quantity of food the petite lady was suddenly consuming. The men subsequently disembarked at a Scandinavian port and von Wolf travelled to Germany, where he joined up as an officer. On 4 September 1916 he was killed at the battle of the Somme. Jayta never returned to Duwisib.

The farm had been allowed to run down during the war and the horses to roam free. (In later

Duwiseb Castle, built in 1908 by Hansheinrich von Wolf (above), *whose first love was horses. In the early 1900s von Wolf established a reputation as a breeder, importing stallions from Europe and crossing them with Afrikaner mares to produce a hardy breed*

years they disappeared and no one seemed to know what happened to them. In 1925 Jayta sold Duwisib to a Swedish farmer called Muurman. She herself lived in Germany and Switzerland, only returning to America after World War II, where she died.

In 1985 I visited Piet van der Westhuizen, who was now working in Walvis Bay. In the course of conversation he referred to some wild horses which lived permanently in the diamond areas of the Namib, and showed me several pictures he had taken. Very few people knew about them, he explained, and even fewer had seen or photographed them. This was largely because they lived in a remote area to which few had access, and CDM had deliberately not publicized their existence as they wanted to discourage ecologists and other well-meaning scientists from wandering around the diamond security area.

Looking at the photographs, I was amazed to see that, despite the desolate setting, they appeared to be in excellent condition, fabulously wild with their long, flowing manes and tails. Piet did not know much about them himself, nor did he know where they had originally come from, but suggested I contacted Chris Eyre, who had been studying them for the Department of Nature Conservation. My imagination thus fired, I contacted Chris, who said he would gladly take me down there if I could obtain the necessary permission to enter the diamond area.

One of the many difficulties of travelling in the Namib is that thousands of square miles are closed to ordinary visitors and tourists. Some areas are closed for conservation reasons (to stop people driving over lychen fields and gravel plains where their tracks could last for seventy years or more). Others are closed for diamond security reasons. Near the coast, for example, it is theoretically possible to pick up diamonds in the desert, so people are dissuaded from going there except under special circumstances. Another reason why the authorities discourage would-be adventurers from entering these areas is their sheer inaccessibility. Very few people are sufficiently well-equipped and experienced to travel in this sort of country and if anything were to go wrong, the consequences could be extremely dire.

Because of the favourable publicity I have been able to offer in the past, and the fact that I am known, and presumably trusted, I have been privileged to visit areas which few outsiders have been to this century. This does not mean that I have always found permits easily obtainable. I have usually had to apply months in advance and have frequently had my applications turned down. Fortunately, my application in 1986 to photograph the wild horses with Chris Eyre (for an article in the London *Sunday Times*) was successful.

In May I met Chris in Southern Namibia and drove west into the Namib with him, heading for an area known as Garub. On the way he told me that since we had last talked he had taken a horse expert, Frans van der Merwe, to see the Garub horses. Van der Merwe had been studying these horses for several years and had an interesting theory about their origins. He had carried out considerable research on the breeds known to have been kept by Baron von Wolf at Duwisib, namely English thoroughbreds, German trakehners, and hackneys crossed with Cape mares. There had been more than three hundred horses at Duwisib before World War I. He and Chris had also talked to the local people who had told them that these horses had been in the Garub area since German times. In his subsequent report van der Merwe had written:

> Geographically Duwisib borders the Namib desert . . . As the crow flies the distance between Duwisib Castle and the present watering place at Garub is about a hundred and fifty kilometres. If the horses were abandoned during the First World War and *did* wander off from Duwisib, they could easily have worked their way south, especially during good rainy seasons, when there would have been drinking water and patches of vegetation along the way.

ABOVE: *'The horses were small but even at a distance there were signs of breeding'*

FOLLOWING PAGES: *Grazing on the eastern side of the desert near Aus*

Van der Merwe now seemed convinced from his observations that they were, at least in part, descended from the Duwisib stock, noting such features as 'the strongly-muscled shoulders with well-defined withers and the generally attractive and characterful heads'.

Garub Mountain is situated between Aus and the coast, about twenty miles into the diamond area. Nearby is another smaller mountain which the Germans called the Klein Tigerberg, and it was here that Chris and I camped beneath an enormous boulder. From the lower slopes of the Tigerberg we had a commanding view over a huge stretch of untamed desert. Although we searched the gravel plains with our binoculars, we saw nothing that first evening, and I wondered how we would ever find the horses in these vast open spaces. Sitting round the fire we talked about our plans for the following day. Where would we be likely to find them and if we did find them how close would we be able to get? There was a full moon that night and the firelight danced on the vertical face of the boulder above us. Earlier Chris had discovered a tampan at the foot of the boulder so we had moved our sleeping-bags out into the open. People have been known to die from the virulent bite of these large ticks.

It was mid-afternoon on the second day when we spotted a herd of six mares and a stallion at the foot of Garub Mountain. They were skirting the lower slopes, heading towards a small group of gemsbok quietly grazing nearby. They saw us coming from far away and galloped off to the north,

ABOVE: *The Garub horses live on coarse, nutritious grasses*

OPPOSITE: *Galloping across the Koichab valley with giant dunes behind*

disappearing over the horizon towards the Koichab valley. We knew we could never catch up with them over that terrain, but followed at our own pace, doubtful that we would see them again. It was just before sunset when we crested a rise and found them grazing only a stone's throw away. They hadn't heard us coming but took off down into the valley the instant we appeared. For a short time we followed, bumping and lurching over tussocks and ridges. I shall never forget seeing those horses thundering across the desolate valley against a backdrop of huge red dunes, their long manes and tails streaming behind, a vision of ultimate freedom.

South-west of our camp was the Garub well or water-point, originally dug to feed the railway line further south, and also to act as a secondary water supply for Luderitz on the coast, before the first desalination plant was constructed there. When the horses came down in World War I they must have found this water-hole and, knowing that they were relying on the supply, CDM have maintained the wind-pump in recent years. This seems to have been due mainly to the initiative of Jan Coetzer of CDM security. A lover of animals, he realized the importance of the water-hole to the horses and persuaded his bosses to provide the necessary funding. Had it not been for him, the wind-pump might easily have fallen into disrepair and the horses would have been forced to move out or die.

The Garub well is the focal point of the horses' four-hundred-square-mile territory, on the western side of the diamond area. In all, they number about two hundred animals, divided into many small breeding herds, with an average size of eight. In many ways their behaviour pattern is identical to that of zebras in the wild. Each herd of mares has its resident stallion, and then there are independent, 'floating' stallions, who continually challenge the herd stallions' supremacy. As young males mature and are weaned from the herd, they automatically join this bachelor pool and begin a 'challenging' existence of constant rivalry. The competition is tough, just as the climatic conditions are harsh.

The American feral horses, which live in a kinder environment, have bred prolifically, causing destruction to their habitat and concern to conservationists. The Namib horses have to withstand blinding sandstorms and temperatures which exceed a hundred and forty degrees Fahrenheit

during the day and then drop to below zero degrees Centigrade at night. Foal mortality is consequently high and the natural conditions appear to maintain their overall number at around two hundred. The animals with which they share the region are the hardiest in the world – oryx, ostrich and springbok – and can go for weeks without water. However, these creatures do not compete with the horses for the sparse grazing in the area, their potential range being far greater and their herds more scattered.

In the evenings, round our camp-fire, Chris and I talked about the Duwisib theory. To us it all seemed extremely plausible, but Chris said that the local people at Aus and Luderitz had other suggestions. Some maintained that the horses had escaped over a period of years from farms that border on the desert, and had joined up into a series of wild herds. One man I later spoke to in Luderitz said that in 1915, the German army was retreating through the Namib when their lines were bombed by the advancing South Africans. In the ensuing chaos, a great many horses are said to have escaped into the desert. Yet another old man told me about a ship from the Argentine that had been wrecked during the diamond rush of 1908–9, just north of the Orange River. This had a cargo of horses on board, many of whom successfully swam ashore and established themselves as a wild herd along the Orange.

Following the publication in 1987 of my article in *The Sunday Times* on these horses, I received a letter from Switzerland from a German couple called Spitzner who used to work at Duwisib, where he was manager after the war.

> I don't know whether you can imagine what a great pleasure it was for Hertha and myself to read the story about the wild horses of the Namib. We are quite convinced that they originate from Duwisib. We remember well the horses that roamed the veld of Duwisib at the time we surveyed the farm. They suddenly disappeared from the farm when the flocks of sheep were enlarged and the veld got drier and drier. When I asked Mr von Kunow Sen what had happened to the horses he evaded a clear answer. I therefore feared that he had shot them all. I was very upset and could never forget about it. It is now the first time I hear about the Namib horses. I feel relieved that Mr von Kunow Sen obviously did not kill the horses, but chased them, maybe with the secret help of neighbours, into the Namib desert. I thank you most heartily for the late relief. Baron von Wolf had imported noble horses from Germany before the First World War for breeding purposes on Duwisib. When the war began, Wolf left SWA [South West Africa] for Germany and was soon killed in France. Nobody took care any more for the breeding horses and they ran wild. How good to know their final fate. Some of them may still have a white pastern on one of their legs passed on to them by a famous stallion that came from a well-known German breed. Hertha and I shall never forget these horses we had loved so dearly.

One of the most interesting stories I heard on my recent travels was the legend of the White Stallion of the Namib, who lived in the dunes south of the Kuiseb. This horse was so beautiful that it captured the imagination of novelists and film-makers alike. Their dream was to film it galloping wildly through the dunes, ghostlike in the fog, caught by the rays of the setting sun. I know two people in Swakopmund who have seen this horse on separate occasions. One of them spoke of a small herd of mares, the stallion's harem, but the older man, Hans Kriess, denied that there were mares as well. He spoke eloquently, however, about the stallion, the vivid memory of which he will carry with him to the grave. He once chanced across it by a water-hole in the dunes, but had no camera with him. Not long after that, during the late 1960s, the stallion was shot by a man who had tried for years to catch it without success. It finally drove him crazy.

PREVIOUS PAGES: *Ostriches, fellow inhabitants of the Sperrgebiet, the forbidden diamond area*

OPPOSITE: *The Sperrgebiet west of Garub, a vast uninhabited wilderness*

CHAPTER SIX

Desert Diamonds

Flying over the desert near Conception Bay in 1985 I spotted some old settlements in a desolate rockscape surrounded by dunes. My pilot told me that he thought they had been abandoned at the time of World War I. Since then no one had been near them. Flying low over one such settlement I saw ox-wagons standing in the sand. Everything seemed just as it had been left all those years ago. Nowhere was there a sign of a road leading in or out. It was this experience that led me to seek special permission from the authorities the following year to visit the settlements by land. Together with Chris Eyre and his colleagues I crossed the desert to Sylvia Hill, on the diamond coast, in order to get there. By sliding our vehicles down seven-hundred-foot dunes we managed to reach the beach and followed it north as far as Meob Bay (see Chapter Three).

I woke next morning to find Chris cursing and swearing at the radio, which obstinately refused to function. Before setting out, he had arranged to contact his office on this particular morning to confirm that all was well. There were many things that could go wrong on a trip like this, and the radio was a precaution – a form of insurance. Now we were neither able to contact the outside world, nor could we ourselves be contacted. Our smart-looking radio was as dead as a dodo. We were on our own.

Setting off again, we headed inland towards the diamond fields. There were no tracks, but we saw beacons (cairns) leading north-east, and assumed that these had been created to signpost the wagon supply route from Meob in the old days. When we found a copper wire lying on the ground, leading in the same direction, we realized that this had probably been the telephone line, the posts having long ago disintegrated. We began to pass heaps of sand and of diamondiferous gravels, and came across our first diamond trommels, where a lonely miner had once waited anxiously for results as his labourers screened the gravel. The trommels are like elongated barrels and were rotated by hand, using a handle at the lower end. A coarse screen, or sieving element, was fitted at the upper end. The gravel was loaded into the top end where the oversize and fine materials were then separated from the 'middlings' (including the diamonds), which passed down through the barrel into a waiting carrying-box at the handle end. These middlings were then taken for hand-sieving in water, where the heavier particles – including diamonds – were separated from the lighter gravel. The resulting refined mixture was then hand-sorted on a table by a trusted employee, or by the 'prospector' himself.

A few miles further on we found the remains of a horse kraal, and a rusted water tank full of sand. There had obviously once been a small community here but the huts had collapsed long ago, with only the roofs now visible above the sand. Beside the kraal was a long horizontal pole where the horses had been tethered, and nearby I found what must have been a rubbish dump, with ox horns, bones and old bottles. It was strange to see how beautiful even a rubbish dump could be. There were no sharp edges any more, no shiny tins or bits of paper, no obtrusive objects. The glass of the bottles had been sand-blasted so that it moulded into the environment. Tins had rusted away

OPPOSITE: *Ghost house in the mining settlement of Holsatia near Conception Bay, where work stopped in the 1920s*

FOLLOWING PAGES: *Ox-wagons abandoned after World War I at Charlottenfelder, near Conception Bay*

CLOCKWISE FROM TOP LEFT: *Chair outside a ghost house, Charlottenfelder; ox graveyard, Charlottenfelder; wheelbarrow and shovel near Pomona; water barrels at Holsatia, once dragged through the dunes behind camels; ox-wagon, Charlottenfelder; shovels abandoned by miners in the 1920s*

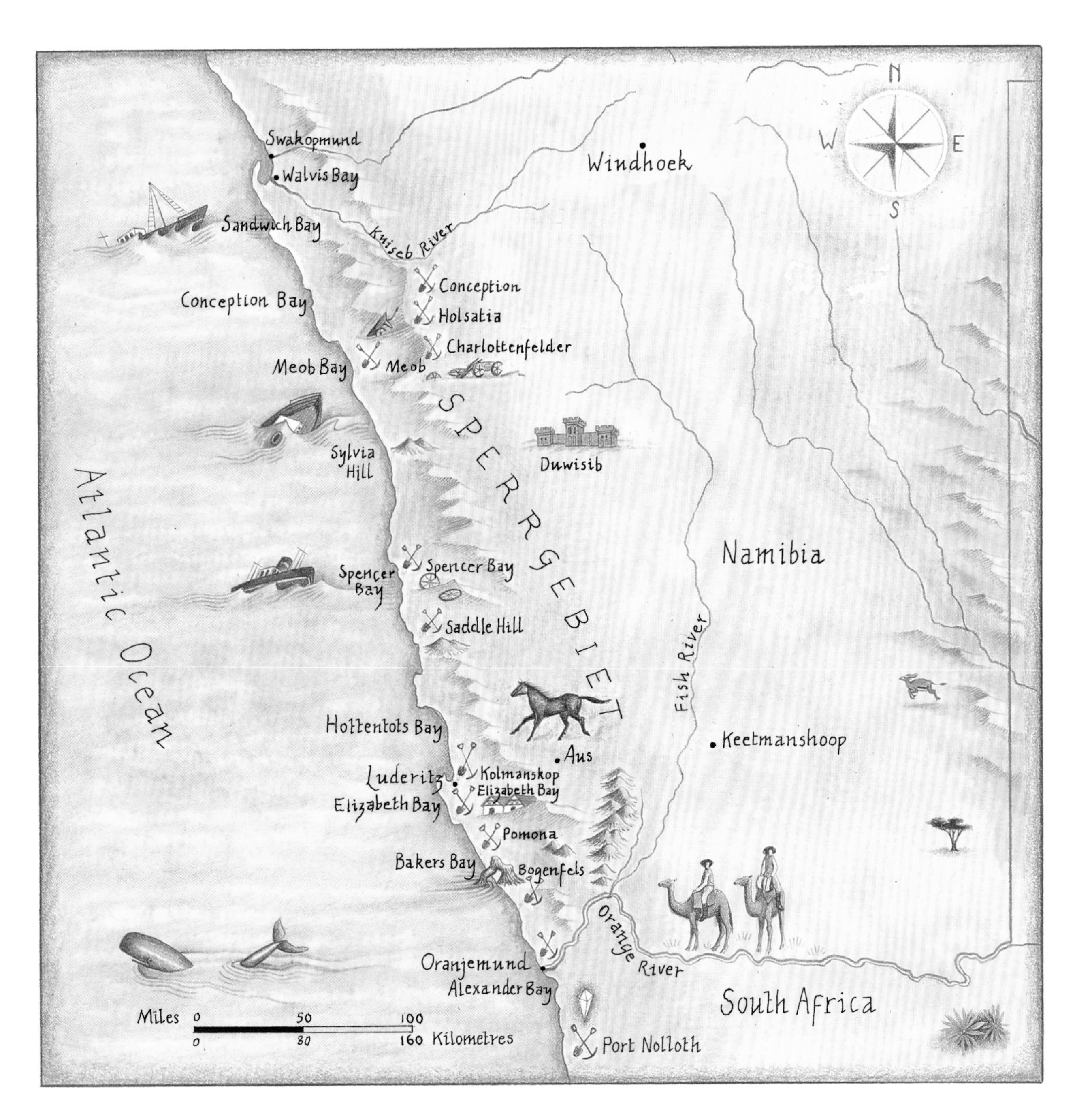

THE DIAMOND COAST

and disappeared, and any paper had long since vanished. The remainder was protected by drifted sand, streaked with mica in the velvet hollows.

From a rocky knoll further on, I studied the horizon with my binoculars. A mile ahead were some wooden structures, and sure enough there was the old workshop I had seen from the air, together with the sorting house, just a skeleton now, and on the left those low shapes would be the ox-wagons I had seen. It was definitely Charlottenfelder, abandoned in the 1920s. I felt a surge of excitement. I had been worried that we might be on the wrong track. It had all looked so easy from the air, yet down here at ground level our view was obscured by dunes and rocky ridges. It would have been quite possible to pass within a mile of the settlement without seeing it, especially if we had been following the wrong beacons. We had seen other lines of beacons going in other directions, but fortunately we had followed the right ones. I had the same feeling I imagine a diver experiences when approaching the wreck of an old ship. This was where the clock stopped all those

Lüderitzbucht (Luderitz Bay) in the 1890s, photographed by the explorer Georg Klinghardt, who later discovered diamonds at Bogenfels (WINDHOEK ARCHIVES)

years ago, when the world was a different place. All sorts of secrets were locked away in those houses. It would be like entering a tomb with ghosts.

Despite the temptation to walk straight into this ghost town, I was aware, as a photographer, that the light was too harsh for me to take good photographs, it being the middle of the day. Instead I skirted round Charlottenfelder, leaving it still untouched, and continued to another settlement further north which I had also flown over in 1985. This was Holsatia which had been abandoned at the same time as Charlottenfelder and Conception (still further north). On the way we stopped to make tea under the slipface of an imposing barchan dune. Barchan dunes are fast-moving crescent-shaped dunes, which form where sand is relatively scarce. They move more or less in line with their two arms, or tentacles, particularly in the direction of the western one, which is always the longer. Because the prevailing wind is from the south-west, the barchans normally move in a north-easterly direction. The northern wall of our dune was sixty feet high, beautifully patterned with long tongues of mica sliding lazily down its precipitous slipface. In the dazzling sunlight the chips of mica looked just like diamonds.

With the light improving, I set off on foot ahead of the others to explore Holsatia. The settlement was more extensive and spread-out than Charlottenfelder. In the foreground was a long line of at least a hundred screening trommels, with the remains of other screening and washing machinery nearby, some of it buried in the sand. In a group to one side I counted eleven of the big water barrels that were dragged through the dunes by camels, the majority in good condition. Most interesting of all though, was a place near the trommels where dozens of shovels stood, handles-up in the sand, just as they had been left when everyone downed tools and abandoned Holsatia in the mid 1920s. Next to the shovels were rows of two-man carrying boxes (with four handles), used to carry the screened stones to the place where final separation was undertaken. Judging from these and the large number of trommels, diamond mining must have been a highly labour-intensive operation, involving a huge workforce.

Climbing the hillside behind the mining area, I found several houses which had presumably

Lüderitzbucht station in 1912 (CDM)

CLOCKWISE FROM TOP LEFT: *The diamond rush of 1908; labourers looking for diamonds in the desert; frenzied excitement as diamonds are found; miners and screening trommels* (WINDHOEK ARCHIVES)

been occupied by the German managers and overseers. Most of the houses had collapsed, like decks of cards, pounded by eighty years of desert winds. One or two sagged dangerously, and looking in through the glassless windows, I saw iron bedsteads protruding from the sand, and sometimes the corner of a table. In another house, a good-looking antique chair stood in an otherwise bare room, with a fine covering of sand. On the mantelpiece were crystal samples, an old scent bottle and part of an oil lamp. In the corner there was a rusty pickaxe, its shaft well-preserved. Chris, who had joined me, saw something sticking out from the sand on the floor – the weathered remains of a notebook with details of mining shifts and the diamonds discovered. The entries were in ink, meticulously written by hand. At the top of the page, which was divided into columns, was the heading 'Namaqua Diamond Company'. The first column gave the number of the field, another the weight of overburden moved and subsequent columns the number of diamonds recovered and their weight in grams, rather than carats. Looking around the room, I half hoped to unearth a dusty jam jar packed with interesting little white stones. Given more time perhaps I would have found one!

Beyond the houses, behind a ridge, were rows and rows of timber A-frames (triangular huts), which because of their design had resisted the elements and looked as if they had only just been built. This was where the long-suffering Owambo labour force would have slept, up to twelve or fifteen to a hut.

Rejoining the others, we drove back to Charlottenfelder, passing a lone ox-wagon on the way, abandoned in the middle of nowhere, its sand-blown woodwork glowing like amber in the last light of day. In Charlottenfelder we camped in an old shed to shelter from the 'south-wester', and fried some clams that we had dug up in the surf the previous evening. After supper I walked out into the night to absorb our surroundings. A crescent moon hung like a Japanese lantern in the sky, and the whole scene glowed with a luminosity that I have only experienced in snow-covered mountains. The combination of white sand and mica was no doubt responsible. It even felt like snow under foot. The night was now completely still, and standing there in the desert silence I found I could hear the Atlantic surf, which I knew was twelve miles away. That distant, ghostly sound gave an added dimension to an atmosphere already charged with the feelings and emotions of a vanished world.

At dawn on the following day, I rose while the others slept and walked over to the five ox-wagons drawn up by the old workshop. Now mostly engulfed by sand, they were no doubt awaiting repairs when everyone left in the 1920s, or perhaps CDM bought them as part of the takeover package and never removed them. A common feature I noticed was the wide metal rim on their wheels, just as people today use wide tyres when driving in sand. Behind the wagons the top of a rusted old bulldozer protruded from the sand, and I wondered if this had sometimes been used to pull these wagons. It was hard to imagine that a team of oxen would have been capable of pulling a laden wagon through dunes. In fact, how had these wagons come here in the first place? They could never have pulled the wagons through the mountainous inland dunes, and there was certainly no question of them having come via the route we had taken. The only other possibility was the coastal route from Walvis Bay, but wagons would surely have been too slow to catch the low tides.

Some months later, I received an answer to these questions when I talked to an old German, Hans Kriess, in Swakopmund. It seemed that Hans's mother worked at these northern settlements in the early days, and he remembered how the miners had taken the wagons down:

OPPOSITE: *Buried machinery at an old mine*

Grasplatz siding, where August Stauch was posted as Bahnmeister (railway supervisor) in 1907. His first job was to keep the railway line free of sand between Kilometres 18 and 27 (from Luderitz)

> They had two or three Hanomag bulldozers with which they towed the wagons along the beach at low tide. With the speed and power of the bulldozers, there was just enough time to get them through before the tide came in. From Walvis Bay they took them overland to Sandwich, and from there to Conception via the 'Langewand' ('long mall' between the dunes and the surf). They also had a special Citroen in those days, with tracks on the back and wide tyres on the front for taking passengers to the diamond fields. It weighed three-quarters of a ton.

Clearly the bulldozer I had seen was one of the Hanomag bulldozers that Hans described.

Hans also told me that the northern fields had been part of the empire of the German millionaire Friedrich Knacke. Knacke had worked at a bank in Hamburg around the turn of the century but was keen to travel and see the world. He had no money so approached the German East Africa Line, who appointed him paymaster on one of their ships. He made his first visit to Luderitz in 1906, and returned there in 1907 with a group of volunteers for the Schutztruppe. That same year he took a job with the Woermann (shipping) Line in Luderitz and was there when August Stauch made his first big diamond discoveries at Kolmanskop (Colman's Hill) near Luderitz in 1908. The story goes that Knacke was a cautious young man, but when he heard a rumour that one prospector at Charlottental, with twenty labourers, was mining a hundred carats a day, he could no longer ignore it. One day he and a friend called Mehrkens, who also worked for Woermann, walked out to the fields and watched the diamonds being washed and sorted from the gravels. This alone was enough to hook Knacke. He succumbed to diamond fever and promptly founded the Woermann Syndicate, applying for prospecting licences.

At first he and Mehrkens were uncertain as to where they should stake their claims. Charlottental appeared to be oversubscribed, so they decided to·try the area near Stauch's claims and agreed to ask his advice. Equipped with shovels, sieves and claim boards they called on him at his camp. Stauch greeted them hospitably and poured them each a large glass of cognac. It was one of those foggy days when the cold and damp chills you to the bone, and they quickly began to thaw out as the fiery liquid percolated through their systems.

'Herr Stauch, we have a few claim boards which we would like to put up somewhere,' said Knacke, and he asked Stauch for any tips as to where diamonds could still be found. 'Have you discovered anything in this area?'

With a smile Stauch took a cigar box from the shelf and handed it to them without saying a word. Knacke opened the box and gasped. It was brim-full of diamonds, and as a shaft of sunlight entered the tent, the stones sparkled before his eyes. They were worth fifteen thousand marks said Stauch. It was a fabulous sight and Knacke could not wait to begin.

The next weekend, he went out to the diamond fields with some members of his new syndicate and began prospecting, which meant crawling around on his stomach, scrutinizing the gravel for little shiny stones. All of a sudden Mehrkens exclaimed, 'Knacke! I have found a diamond!' It was a beautiful pure stone, a perfect octahedron. Within a short time they had found a number of other stones. The Woermann Syndicate was in business. Some months later, Knacke sold an option on his claims for one and a half million marks, a lot of money in those days. He had taken his first steps on a path that would lead him to fame and fortune.

In September that year, the German Government imposed a variety of restrictions on the diamond producers, which barred them from staking any new claims in the desert area between the Orange River in the south and the twentieth latitude south in the north. This was known as the Sperrgebiet Decree, when the forbidden area was first proclaimed. The boundaries of this area were subsequently extended in the 1920s to cover the area between the twenty-sixth latitude and Walvis Bay.

Under the terms of the 1908 decree, the German Government was granted the sole right to prospect and mine in this area, only a few producers like Stauch and Knacke receiving prior recognition for having duly reported their claims before the government decrees came in. Consequently several of the Luderitz producers, particularly those whose southern claims had not been recognized by the government, turned their attention to the northern area, between Luderitz and Walvis Bay. It was then that discoveries were made – at Spencer Bay in December 1908 and at Meob, Charlottenfelder, Holsatia and Conception in early 1909. Knacke was one of the producers who became interested in the northern fields, most of which were later consolidated under the controlling umbrella of his Namaqua Diamond Company of South West Africa, which he founded just after World War I. This was also one of the companies which later exploited the immensely rich terraces south of the Orange River mouth, the most profitable diamond venture he ever made.

Unlike Stauch, Knacke also diversified successfully, moving into such fields as platinum, stockbroking, property, fishing and mining engineering. One of his companies was Atlantic Engineering Works which, amongst other products, made all the bearings for the screening equipment on the diamond fields. Platinum, however, was Knacke's most lucrative venture. He made a fortune from Hans Merensky's platinum discoveries in the Transvaal, South Africa, and floated a company, Lydenberg Platinum Areas, in London. He had a yacht and a beautiful property in the Cape, where he eventually retired.

PREVIOUS PAGES AND ABOVE: *Sand-dunes overwhelming a Kolmanskop house*

The diamond fields near Meob and Conception Bay were never very profitable compared to his other ventures. The size of the stones in the northern fields had always been inferior to those further south, nearer the Orange. With the deepening recession in the late 1920s, Knacke sold out to Ernest Oppenheimer's newly-formed Consolidated Diamond Mines of South West Africa, which by now controlled almost the entire Sperrgebiet, north and south. Conception, Charlottenfelder, Holsatia and Meob were finally abandoned, with their diamonds, to the wind and sands.

The most sensational diamond discoveries were made by Stauch in 1908 and 1909 near Luderitz. These finds took the world completely by surprise. In the early 1900s, diamonds in Africa were mainly associated with Cecil Rhodes's Kimberley in South Africa, and with 'blue ground', otherwise known as kimberlite. If there was no blue ground, it was said, there could be no diamonds because kimberlite, a type of lava, was the 'host rock' for diamonds. Hardest of all known stones, diamonds were formed millions of years ago, when subterranean fragments of carbon were trapped in molten lava that was forced to the earth's surface under tremendous pressure. When searching for diamonds, the first thing that geologists looked for was kimberlite. Since there was no known kimberlite in Namibia, nobody had thought of looking for diamonds. Thus, when the first discoveries were made, most geologists and mining engineers received the news with scepticism.

August Stauch was a railway engineer of humble origins, who came to work in Namibia for health reasons. An asthmatic, he accepted a transfer to the dry, sunny German colony, because he was advised by his boss, for whom he had great respect, that it might be good for him. His employers were under contract to extend the railway from Aus, at the edge of the Namib, to Keetmanshoop further east, and the section from Luderitz to Aus had only recently been opened. Although he had only just married, and accepting the transfer meant a two-year separation, he and his wife Ida decided that he should take the opportunity, which might lead to a better and healthier life for them both. He booked a passage on the *Windhuk*, and set a course to wealth *and* health.

After leaving the lushness of springtime Germany one can imagine his first impressions on arriving at Luderitz Bay. It would be hard to visualize a bleaker and more desolate setting than this dusty German town on the Atlantic side of the Namib. I remember my own first visit there in 1976, when I camped by the water's edge and woke the next morning to a cold, grey dawn. In the distance, across the bay, I could see grey dunes and bare rockscapes beneath the fog blanket, which hung oppressively over the Atlantic waters. 'Is this really Africa?' I remember asking myself. I thought then, as I have often reflected since, of the hardships the diamond hunters must have endured in those diamond fields.

Stauch was luckier than me (in more senses than one) in that he arrived on a cold sunny day, and was therefore able to take in some of the finer points of his surroundings. He was met by his employer's representative, and several days later took up his new position as railway supervisor (Bahnmeister) at Grasplatz, about fifteen miles east of Luderitz. His first job was to keep the railway line free of sand between Kilometres 18 and 27 (from Luderitz). The strong south-westerly winds were forever blowing the sand over the lines, and Stauch had a gang of labourers whom he deployed along this section. The name of his new home–'grassy place' – was a joke, in that not a blade of grass grew within fifty miles of it. He settled in quickly though, and because of his varied interests, which included walking in the dunes and studying nature as well as socializing in Luderitz, he soon began to enjoy life.

The geology of the desert began to interest Stauch, too, and he started collecting stones, such as coloured agates, of which there were plenty. Then he took out two prospecting licences from the Deutsche Kolonialgesellschaft (the DKG), and asked his men to bring him any pretty stones which they found. He even said in jest, 'And look out especially for diamonds,' at which everyone laughed because they all knew that diamonds were only found in the blue ground. Two weeks after this, however, one of the labourers, Zacharias Lewala, saw something shiny in the sand while he was shovelling, and picked up a tiny white stone. With the words, 'Mister, 'n mooi klip' ('Sir, a pretty stone'), he handed it to the foreman, who sent a message to Stauch to say that an interesting stone had been found. Stauch tested the stone on the glass of his wrist-watch when he arrived, and when it cut the glass, became convinced that they had found a diamond.

He pegged his claims in the area where the stone had been found, and promptly applied to the DKG for more prospecting licences. He also resigned from his job as Bahnmeister and persuaded his two bosses in Luderitz, Sönke Nissen and Max Weidtmann, to give him financial backing. Both Weidtmann and Nissen were subsequently to become extremely wealthy as a result of their decision to do so. Laboratory tests soon confirmed that Stauch's stone, and others that followed, were not only diamonds, but gemstones of exceptional quality, water-clear and nearly flawless.

When the first diamond was discovered in April 1908, Stauch immediately realized the importance of keeping the find quiet, and impressed the same on his colleagues. It was, of course, known in Luderitz that he was prospecting in the desert, but nobody took that too seriously, simply labelling him as a bit of a crank. Then stories began to circulate that Stauch had discovered diamonds, but most people were merely amused and dismissed them out of hand. Even when, for

example, he took his first stones in to the new Bergtechnisches laboratory in Swakopmund for confirmation, the laboratory official was initially unimpressed, telling him that diamonds were not the only stones around that would cut glass. Everyone's scepticism worked in Stauch's favour, giving him nearly two clear months to peg the best claims for himself.

What finally made Stauch's sceptics sit up was when he began to give away diamonds in large quantities. People gathered in bars and at street corners to hear the news. Surely, they reasoned, Stauch must have considerable numbers of stones if he was able to give away so many. If he had amassed these reserves in such a short time, his prospecting could no longer just be pure 'moonshine'. Then came confirmation from the government geologist, Dr Paul Range. His report stated that accident was the best prospector – for over twenty years ox-wagons had trundled up and down this route, with increased military traffic during the Hottentot uprisings, yet no one had noticed the diamonds with which the route was paved.

The Range report tipped the scales and the rush was on. Every able-bodied man in Luderitz equipped himself with an enamel basin, a wire sieve, a shovel and a broom, and headed out to the diamond fields, bringing the town to a standstill. The news spread like wildfire and fortune-seekers converged on Luderitz in ox-wagons, carts and whatever other transport they could find. Hotels and lodgings bulged at the seams. Fresh water was at a premium – it soon became cheaper to have a bath in soda water – and most of it was imported by steamer from Cape Town on a weekly basis, and also by rail from the water-point at Garub, where the wild horses now drink.

The British prospector, Fred Cornell, visited Luderitz during this period and later wrote, in his book, *The Glamour of Prospecting* (first published in 1920):

> With the discovery of diamonds came the influx of 'all sorts and conditions of men' usual to 'rushes' all over the world, and water rose to famine prices. Washing in sea water, when tried by a few over-particular new chums, was followed by extremely painful results, for the brine aggravated a hundredfold the painful sun-blisters inevitable in a country where the blazing rays of a sub-tropical sun beat back with redoubled fierceness from the glaring, scorching, all-pervading sand. A helmet, whilst absolutely essential, is after all but little protection from a glare that comes from the sand all around one as from a huge mirror. We soon found that, if this glare was to be borne at all, it was by using spectacles of smoked glass and these, fitted with wire gauze side-protectors, are also essential in the blinding sandstorms that form a frequent variation of Luderitz weather conditions.
>
> We found the place so crowded that it was almost impossible to obtain even the roughest accommodation; the hotels were full, the stores were full, every shanty dignified by the name of a dwelling was crammed, men 'pigging it' four and six in tiny rooms meant for a single occupant, and food, and above all water, at famine prices.
>
> So great had been the rush, for a time, that the police had been quite unable to cope with it, and when I came to see more of the motley crowd of 'fortune seekers' that had invaded the place, I easily forgave the irascibility of the stout, overfed and overheated German officials who had had to deal with them all. What a lot they were! Only a small minority were genuine prospectors, engineers, or mining men with a legitimate interest in the diamond discoveries; the majority were shady 'company promoters', bucket-shop experts, warned-off bookmakers and betting men ('brokers' they usually styled themselves), and sharpers of all sorts, on the look-out for prey in the shape of

OPPOSITE: *'It was eerie walking through those empty rooms. Sand had drifted high in some corners and most of the window panes had long since been shattered by sandstorms'*

Prinzenbucht was used as a port and occasional source of supply for Pomona and Bogenfels when weather conditions allowed. Ships would anchor offshore, and passengers and goods were brought ashore in surf boats (WINDHOEK ARCHIVES)

> lucky diggers or discoverers. Then, too, there were a number of self-styled 'prospectors', runaway ships' cooks, stewards, stokers, and sea men, the bulk of whom had never seen a rough diamond in their lives, and of course a modicum of genuine men of past experience – principally ex 'river-diggers' – men whose small capital was running away like water for bare necessities in this miserable dust-hole of creation.

In those early months many people simply crawled over the desert on their stomachs, picking up diamonds with the blade of a knife and putting them in a small tin, which they hung around their necks for safety. I can remember hearing an interview with an old woman who described how labourers were sent out to the fields with a jam jar and a broom, to return later in the day, the jars blazing with diamonds. Young men would give presents of diamonds to ladies they fancied, and payment for a wide variety of services was made in diamonds instead of cash. At the bar in Kapps' Hotel, for instance, someone would call 'Kapps, I want to pay,' whereupon Kapps would produce a cigar box from which he took a small set of scales. The weights were placed at one end and the diamonds at the other, until the scales balanced. The account was thus settled. He used to reckon one carat as equalling twenty marks. All this changed, though, when the Sperrgebiet Decree of September 1908 made it illegal for diamonds to be given away or traded unofficially. All stones would now have to be registered within twenty-four hours of discovery, or become illegal. It is still illegal to be in possession of an uncut diamond in Namibia today.

As mining operations expanded, life on the diamond fields became glamorous and flamboyant. There were dance evenings, theatre evenings and fancy-dress balls, with themes such as 'Gypsy Evening' and 'A Night in Venice'. People dressed fashionably in clothes imported from Paris and Berlin. Ostrich-feather boas were then *de rigueur* and on special occasions the gentlemen wore black ties, stiff collars, top hats and spats. The bars opened early, and champagne was imported from Europe and taken on to the more distant fields by ox-wagon. Champagne breakfasts were popular in Luderitz, and Kapps's chandeliers were irresistible targets to sharpshooters in jubilant mood after a good day on the fields. Uniformed waiters would simply jot down 'one chandelier' on their bar bill. There were more in Kapps's store. Horse racing became a popular sport and a Racing Club was founded in 1909 – the 'Lüderitzbuchter Rennverein'. Race meetings were held at weekends, and special meetings were organized for visiting German ships. Race-horses were purchased for enormous sums, sometimes imported from the Cape and sometimes from well-known breeders like von Wolf at Duwisib.

The most sensational diamond discovery in the Namib, which was also the most spectacular discovery the world has ever known, occurred on New Year's Eve 1908, when most people were celebrating in the bars of Luderitz. A visiting professor, Dr Scheibe, from the Royal Mining Academy in Berlin, had recently arrived in Luderitz in order to meet Stauch and see the 'Diamond King's' fields for himself. He and Stauch got on well from the start, and Stauch invited him to join him on a prospecting expedition to an area south of Luderitz opposite Pomona Island.

The cemetery at Pomona

It took them most of that December day to reach the area, and in the afternoon their way was blocked by a huge sand-dune which they struggled vainly to cross. Their labourers began to complain, but in the end they succeeded and Stauch named the valley beyond Idatal, after his wife Ida. Here they made camp and Scheibe immediately went off into another valley in search of stones, already smitten with 'diamond fever'. Stauch himself walked west towards the coast in order to plot their position as accurately as possible on the map. On his return he found one of his employees, Jakob, carrying driftwood for the fire. He jokingly said to him, 'Don't look for wood, Jakob, look for diamonds.' Jakob, who did not understand Stauch's sense of humour, dropped the driftwood and got down on his knees, thinking his boss was serious. Immediately he began picking up diamonds from round their feet, in such numbers that he soon had to cram a handful into his mouth as he had no pockets in his trousers. Stauch called out to Scheibe, who ran over and gasped in amazement at the unbelievable spectacle. As Stauch and Jakob picked up diamonds as fast as they could, he started crying repeatedly, 'Ein Märchen! Ein Märchen!' (A fairy-tale! A fairy-tale!)

This valley thus became known as Märchental (fairy-tale valley), which of course it was – Scheibe was later to describe the diamonds as 'lying like plums under a tree'. By this time the light was failing and they were forced to return to their camp, where they sat round the fire discussing the extraordinary events of that evening: a fitting end to an extraordinary year. Later the moon rose, flooding the valley in silvery light, and they could not resist the temptation to return to the valley and make sure it had not all been a dream. They walked over the hill and, sure enough, there were the diamonds, glittering in the moonlight, like a scene from the Arabian Nights. This was the richest diamond discovery ever made, and the valley was later described as being 'as thickly studded with lustrous gems as the showcases in a jeweller's window'.

Early in 1989, I had the rare privilege of driving through Idatal and Märchental, accompanied by a security officer from CDM. Never in my life have I seen such colours as glowed from the rocks of these valleys, as rich a blend of African golds and reds as you could ever imagine. But by the time the diamond fields were closed down in the 1920s, they had been swept bare of surface gravels and diamonds, so that now you have to be lucky to pick up a diamond. The narrow-gauge railway down Idatal has virtually disintegrated after seventy years of fog and neglect, and August Stauch's headquarters, known as 'Stauch's Laager', has been all but razed to the ground by the elements. The foundations of the buildings were still in evidence and I was shown the narrow torpedo cubicles where the labourers slept. There were also some iron beds, which the Germans must have used, and the kitchen chimneys standing like monuments to a lost world.

That evening we camped in Pomona, the ghost town that sprang up as a result of Stauch's finds, but which was subsequently abandoned in 1929 some years after the takeover by Ernest Oppenheimer's Anglo American Corporation and the subsequent formation of the new Consolidated Diamond Mines of South West Africa. Only a handful of visitors have been allowed here since that time. I found the town standing just as it had been left. The German manager's house had been built high up on a rocky ridge overlooking the valley, with the labourers' quarters far below, giving him a definite psychological advantage. Near the quarters was the old plant, its machinery partly buried by drifted sand, and scattered around were various relics of the old days. Wheelbarrows and shovels lay frozen in time, untouched in seventy years. The wheels and cab of a stylish horse gig protruded from a dune, the type which ladies used to travel to the races. A little out of town, beyond the manager's house, was Pomona's old cemetery, set in the bleakest landscape imaginable. Since most of the inscriptions were originally carved or painted on wood, they have long since disappeared through decades of sand-blasting. Only one or two epitaphs engraved on stone have survived the test of time.

Ghost houses at Kolmanskop

We slept on the verandah of the manager's house, which bore the inscription 'POMONA 1912'. Earlier, at sunset, I had walked through its empty rooms feeling like a ghost myself, as shafts of light fell on dusty brass doorhandles and carved fireplaces. Sand had drifted high in the corners, and most of the window panes had long ago been shattered by sandstorms. Lying on the verandah at midnight, I watched the moon rise over the desert, adding to the ghostly atmosphere, and I half expected to hear the muffled chime of a grandfather clock, or the sound of a distant accordion.

In the diamond days everything had to be imported, including water. There was nothing at Pomona, just empty tracts of desert. Sailors who were wrecked here in earlier times had little chance of survival. In *Lords of the Last Frontier*, Lawrence Green tells a story of a German surgeon called Rogge, who in 1905 set off on horseback from Luderitz with a 'Schutztruppler' (colonial trooper) called Friebecke. They were carrying mail and pay for the men at a lonely outpost beyond. According to Green, they both disappeared, and it was not until 1911 that Friebecke's belt and bayonet were discovered in the dunes. The search was renewed, and in 1912 a patrol found Rogge's body with the money, about two thousand marks, still on him. The mail was also found in his bag

ABOVE: *Luderitz today*

OPPOSITE: *Bullet-ridden old sign at the edge of the Sperrgebiet (forbidden diamond area)*

and delivered seven years later. In his pocket notebook he had written a farewell letter to his mother and sister in Germany: 'The horses have run away, I have lost touch with Friebecke, and to avoid death from thirst I am going to shoot myself.' Friebecke's body was not found until 1928. According to Green, he was buried in Luderitz with full military honours, after lying out in the desert for nearly a quarter of a century.

The next day we left Pomona and drove south to Bogenfels, meaning arched rock, a ghost diamond town that took its name from the two-hundred-foot natural rock arch on the wild coastline nearby. Not long after Stauch's discoveries near Luderitz, the explorer and prospector Georg Klinghardt remembered that he had seen some stones on one of his trips which might possibly have been diamonds. Encouraged by friends, he organized an expedition with camels to check on this possibility, and finally arrived at the Bogenfels, recognizing it as the place he remembered. His memory had served him well. Searching the area he soon found many large stones of high quality in the vicinity of the arch and a little mining town sprang up to exploit these riches. But Klinghardt was not involved in the mining phase. Although he could easily have made a fortune from the stones he picked up, he was scrupulously honest and duly handed over the initial fortune he had discovered to his employers. (Some 400,000 carats of diamonds were removed from the desert at Bogenfels between 1910 and 1913.) There were also other occasions on the diamond fields when he could easily have become a millionaire, but instead he retired on a modest pension. He was never financially ambitious, his greatest desire being to travel to remote places where no other man had trod. He was an extraordinarily gifted photographer and took the first high-quality photographs to come out of the area.

Not everyone in those days was as honest as Klinghardt. Security was a major headache for the authorities in Luderitz, even after the Sperrgebiet Decree. Before the decree there was nothing to stop someone possessing an uncut diamond or trading it like cash, or giving it away, so long as he had a valid prospecting licence. At that time it was estimated that as many as half the diamonds being recovered from the desert were later stolen. Initially only two policemen were stationed at Kolmanskop, and they were responsible for security throughout the diamond fields. The uniformity of the Luderitz diamonds was such that there was often no way of proving where they had come from. Over millions of years the sea and wind had effectively graded them into groups of similar size and shape. If someone stole some stones from another individual or from someone else's claims, he could always argue that the stones came from his own claim. For the same reasons 'salting' was a frequent problem. When someone wished to sell his claims, having himself found no stones on them, he would sprinkle a few over his barren fields, like salt from a cellar. He would then proudly show prospective buyers round, leading them to the places where he had sprinkled the stones. Seeing the number of diamonds, the buyers would be impressed, imagining the fields to be extremely rich.

After Stauch's finds at Märchental (Pomona), it was discovered that the mineral rights for the entire area opposite Pomona Island, including the valleys of Idatal and Märchental, had already been granted to De Pass and Spence in the Cape during the previous century, long before anyone knew that diamonds would be found there. The news inevitably came as a massive shock to Stauch, who had, of course, wasted no time in pegging claims in the valleys. When the news of his Pomona discoveries had first reached Luderitz there was pandemonium, as prospectors tore off to Pomona taking horses, camels, provisions and claim boards. They were thus equally shattered by the news that the diamonds were not theirs to mine.

De Pass and Spence were guano miners in the nineteenth century, and signed a treaty with the Hottentot Chief, David Christian, at Bethanie in 1863. By the terms of the treaty with Christian,

they were granted rights for the coastal strip between Baker's Bay and Luderitz (then Angra Pequeña). Then Adolf Lüderitz arrived and the German flag was hoisted at Angra Pequeña, whereupon De Pass vigorously complained to Britain. The British Government, in turn, protested to the German Government, and a series of diplomatic moves took place between the two governments. As a result, two Anglo-German commissions of enquiry were set up in the late nineteenth century and these ruled that De Pass and Spence & Co should be granted 'for themselves and their assigns a full title in perpetuity to the Pomona mine with two English miles round the mine on every side'. No one at the time thought that they were being excessively generous in giving De Pass the Pomona mine.

All these complications effectively delayed the legal opening of Pomona for three and a half years. During this period an army of lawyers beavered away trying to sort out the mess, until eventually De Pass's descendant in London was persuaded to sell his rights. While the negotiations dragged on, everyone knew that there were diamonds galore within a day's journey of Luderitz, but that they were illegal. Prospectors were explicitly forbidden to pick them up until the dispute was resolved, but the temptation to organize illicit expeditions was immense. Security was minimal and the story goes that the injunction was often quietly ignored.

The Sperrgebiet Decree of 1908 closed many security loopholes, but illicit diamond dealing continued, rather like tax evasion, as a popular sport. For instance, despite the laws which required prospectors to deposit diamonds at the bank within twenty-four hours of discovery, the 'good-time girls' at the Greenhouse brothel were more often than not still paid in diamonds. In fact, the Greenhouse seems to have acquired a reputation for being a hotbed of 'IDB' (Illicit Diamond Buying). The story goes that the Madame of the brothel, Frau Zimmer, had a fierce dog which she kept in a kennel in her yard. Unknown to the police, the kennel had a double wall, and she hid her illicit stones in the space between. Other tricks included boxes with false bottoms, shoes with special cavities inside the heels, and the age-old hiding-place below the floorboards. Some of the chancers were successful, but others fell victim to informers when they came to sell their illicit wares.

The 'good old days' lasted until the outbreak of war in August 1914, when mining ceased abruptly by order of the Governor, Dr Seitz. All able-bodied men were called up in readiness for the expected invasion from South Africa, which took place within weeks of war having been declared. Luderitz itself was occupied in September 1914, without a shot being fired, and many of the inhabitants were interned, some in a camp at nearby Aus. The fighting in South West Africa was only to last a year. The Germans were hopelessly out-numbered by the British and South Africans, and eventually surrendered to their invaders on 9 July 1915. That same year, in September, mining was started again at Luderitz, though on a different basis. Elsewhere the war was still raging, so the mines were only allowed to operate on a limited scale, with a monthly quota of ten thousand carats each. The diamonds were to be deposited at a South African bank and a payment of one pound per carat was made in the form of a loan to the respective miners. It was not a profitable arrangement, but at least the people had jobs and income.

The Treaty of Versailles in 1918, which marked the end of World War I, officially stripped Germany of her African colonies. South West Africa (Namibia) was henceforth to be administered by the South Africans in terms of the League of Nations mandate. After 1918, the former colony was left to continue as it had been before the war, in most respects, but some of the diamond producers were nervous that South Africa might expropriate their mines. Encouraged by his lawyer, Erich Lübbert, who also represented other producers, Stauch and his fellow 'Diamond Kings' decided that it would be safer for them to consolidate their interests and ally themselves with a major South

African producer, provided it could be on their own terms. Lübbert acted as the go-between, and found a willing buyer in Ernest Oppenheimer and his recently founded Anglo American Corporation. As a result of Lübbert's initiative, the independence of the South West African Diamond Mines came to an end, and in January 1920 the Consolidated Diamond Mines of South West Africa (CDM) was born in Cape Town. Stauch and the other producers received three and a half million pounds, half in cash and the rest in shares in the new company.

The early 1920s saw all the independent producers gradually fused into the new organization, normally referred to by employees as 'The Company'. Meanwhile work continued at Kolmanskop and Pomona, and also at Elizabeth Bay, where a massive new processing plant opened in 1926. Diamond production returned to its pre-war levels and then news arrived of the spectacular discoveries south of the Orange, an area where Knacke was already involved. In just one month the geologists Hans Merensky and Ernst Reuning had dug up nearly seven thousand beautiful diamonds, worth millions of pounds at today's value, in a small area just south of the river mouth. One stone alone weighed 71.1 carats, a magnificent blue gemstone.

The key to Merensky and Reuning's successes was their superior understanding of how the diamonds had ended up on the Namib sands, close to the coast, though the two had different theories. Merensky had for some time argued that the diamonds had offshore origins, having been

PREVIOUS PAGES: *Abandoned buildings on the diamond coast at Hottentots Bay, not far from Saddle Hill*

BELOW: *Foggy morning at Elizabeth Bay. In the background is the old casino*

Mural in a house at Elizabeth Bay. The story goes that a German miner advertised in Germany for a wife, describing a tropical scene with palm trees where he lived. On arrival, his disillusioned fiancée complained about the total absence of trees, whereupon he pointed to the wall, saying: 'Here they are, my dear'

washed ashore from an unknown diamond pipe on the sea-bed. Reuning, on the other hand, argued that the diamonds had come from rich inland pipes (ie. blue ground) in the Southern African interior, whence they had been washed by tributaries into the Orange River system. Eventually they were swept down to the Atlantic and carried back on to the shore by the strong current. Merensky would not accept this theory because, he maintained, if the diamonds had come from an inland source, then there must be diamonds upstream on the banks of the river itself. Yet none had been found. This argument was later to fall away when diamonds were discovered up the Orange, and today Reuning's theory is upheld as being correct.

On the Namib coast, both the current and the prevailing wind come from the south west. Over millions of years both sand and diamonds have been washed down the Orange system and then deposited by the sea on the coastline, mainly north of the river. When the coastline changed and beaches became raised, the sand was blown north-east by the wind into the Namib interior. This was the origin of the Namib sands – the great sand sea. The smaller diamonds were also blown by gale-force winds, carried along by the sand, and the smaller the diamonds, the further they went. At Meob and Conception, four hundred miles north of the Orange, the stones were smaller than those near Luderitz, rarely more than half a carat in weight. Having come down the Orange, the bigger stones remained close to the river, too heavy to be carried by the wind. The reason for the remarkable accumulation of stones near Luderitz is thought to be due to the lie of the land. Both diamonds and sand reaching the coast at Elizabeth Bay were 'funnelled' north into a narrow series of valleys leading to Kolmanskop. The same was true further south at Pomona, explaining the richness of those fields. Much of this had been guessed by Stauch. Early on, for instance, he realized

Coloured (uncut) diamonds, known as 'fancies' (CDM)
A fortune in uncut diamonds (CDM)

Narrow-gauge railway near Marchental, Pomona, scene of the most spectacular diamond discoveries the world has ever known

that the diamonds were always to be found in the valleys, and not on the hills. He had also guessed that the diamonds had come from the south, but neither he nor his fellow producers had grasped the broader picture.

Although Merensky stuck to his offshore pipe theory, he did realize as early as 1908 when he first visited the Luderitz fields, having been commissioned by the South African mines to investigate the new discoveries, that there was a definite correlation between the occurrence of diamonds and the ancient raised beaches recognized by their warm-water oyster shells. He was later able to prove his theory at Alexander Bay with Reuning in 1927. When he saw the old fossil shells there, he knew he was in the right place. It was this understanding, amongst other qualities, that made him a millionaire and one of the most famous geologists of his day.

The large horn-shaped shell belongs to a warm-water species of oyster, *Ostrea prismatica*, normally only found on Indian Ocean shores. Today these oysters do not exist on the west coast, but Merensky believed that many thousands of years ago, the warm Indian Ocean current had flowed round the Cape and up the west coast, bringing the oysters with it. At that time, he suggested, the Cape Peninsula was an island, and the warm current flowed uninterrupted across the 'Cape flats' and up the west coast. At some stage the flats silted up and the warm waters were forced to find their way around the peninsula, where they were blocked by the Atlantic. Thus the supply of warm water was cut off and the oysters died, frozen by the icy Benguela waters. The shells were left high and dry on the old shores and I have often seen them, miles inland, lying on the desert after being uncovered by the shifting sands. They are large and reddish-pink, about the size of a man's hand, and flat like a normal oyster shell. They can be exquisitely beautiful, sculpted by centuries of wind-blown sand.

CDM were watching Merensky and Reuning with great interest. Up to now they had regarded the discoveries south of the Orange as probably being unconnected with their fields, even though the diamonds might originally have shared a common source. A number of geologists had already prospected on the north bank of the river and found little, but when CDM heard that Merensky's diamonds were not all found near the surface but had been dug up from a trench, they decided to have another look. In mid-1927 they sent their geologists from Kolmanskop to prospect in the area. These men went further than their predecessors by moving large overburdens of sand, and they subsequently made discoveries which eclipsed anything hitherto imaginable.

With these new finds, and with the ominous rumblings of a gathering world depression, CDM began to close down all their northern (less economic) operations, and to concentrate on the rich fields north of the Orange River mouth. A new security town was established called Oranjemund (Orange mouth) just north of Alexander Bay, which became the headquarters of CDM's mining operations, as it is today. The old settlements, their treasure reaped, became ghost towns in the forbidden area which no one was permitted to enter. Ravaged by wind and sand, the walls crumbled and collapsed and the machinery rusted away into grotesque monuments of engineering. Only Daliesque scenes of skeleton houses and wind-battered graveyards in a setting of utter desolation are left to remind us of those glamorous old days.

FOLLOWING PAGES: *Elizabeth Bay*

BELOW: *Remains of an ox-wagon, relic of a vanished world*

CHAPTER SEVEN

The Skeleton Coast

About fifteen years ago, I was shown an aerial photograph of a bay on the Skeleton Coast, with a mountain rising sheer from the beach, and a shipwreck lying in two parts at the foot of the cliffs. Behind and beyond was a desolate backdrop of dunes and mountains, in contrast to the dark blue rollers and breakers near the shore. In the middle of the bay was a rocky island against which the seas broke in a perpetual welter of foam. Never in my wildest dreams had I imagined such a scene.

Several years passed before I discovered that the picture I had admired was of Spencer Bay, a hundred and fifty miles south of Walvis Bay and one of the most inaccessible spots on the whole Namib coastline. The mountain itself was Dolphin Head and the island Mercury Island. I longed to go there, yet in those days, for me, it was out of the question. Most people I talked to had never heard of it, and the handful that had shook their heads. They knew of no one who had been there. It was impossible to approach by sea because of the great distances and exceptionally heavy surf. To go by vehicle was also not feasible because of the huge dunes, and this only left a helicopter as an option. The chances of obtaining permission to get into the Sperrgebiet were remote, even if I could have afforded a six-hundred-mile round trip in a helicopter.

In 1986 I was in the Namib, taking photographs for another article. I needed aerial pictures of the coast and two friends (Victor Hugo and Martin Louw, both pilots) flew directly to the desert to help with my assignment. I requested permission to land at Spencer Bay and, to my excitement, this was granted, provided we could find a safe landing place. Early one morning we took off from Luderitz in a Cessna Centurion, and flew north along the diamond coast on a cloudless, though windy day. We passed over Hottentots Bay, Gibraltar Rock, and the abandoned mining settlements at Saddle Hill, and then Spencer Bay came into view. As a landmark, Dolphin Head is easily recognizable, being the highest point on the coast between Table Mountain (Cape Town) and 'Namibe' (previously Mossamedes) in Angola, a distance of nearly fifteen hundred miles. Circling the mountain we looked directly down at the wreck of the *Otavi*, a steamer which came to grief there in 1945. Near the bow section was a colony of at least a thousand fur seals. From the air it looked very dramatic and exciting, and we searched for a place to land. There was a large open area of sand just east of Dolphin Head, so we flew low over it trying to assess the surface for a possible safe landing. The difficulty was how to judge whether it was hard enough to land on. The sandy flats in question might be liable to flooding after high tides, so how could we be certain it was safe now? It could be hard on the surface, but soft underneath. Our aircraft also needed a sufficient length of sand on which to land. We were confident that it was enough, but the Centurion is heavy and the wheels can easily dig themselves in. The temptation to risk it was enormous: we were dying to land and explore, but our priority had to be safety, and we dared not compromise in a situation like this. We had tried to land in the desert the previous day and knew how close we had come to getting stuck. Very reluctantly we decided to abandon our attempt and return to our base at Luderitz.

OPPOSITE: *Remains of the* Tong Wha, *a Korean vessel wrecked near Spencer Bay in 1972*

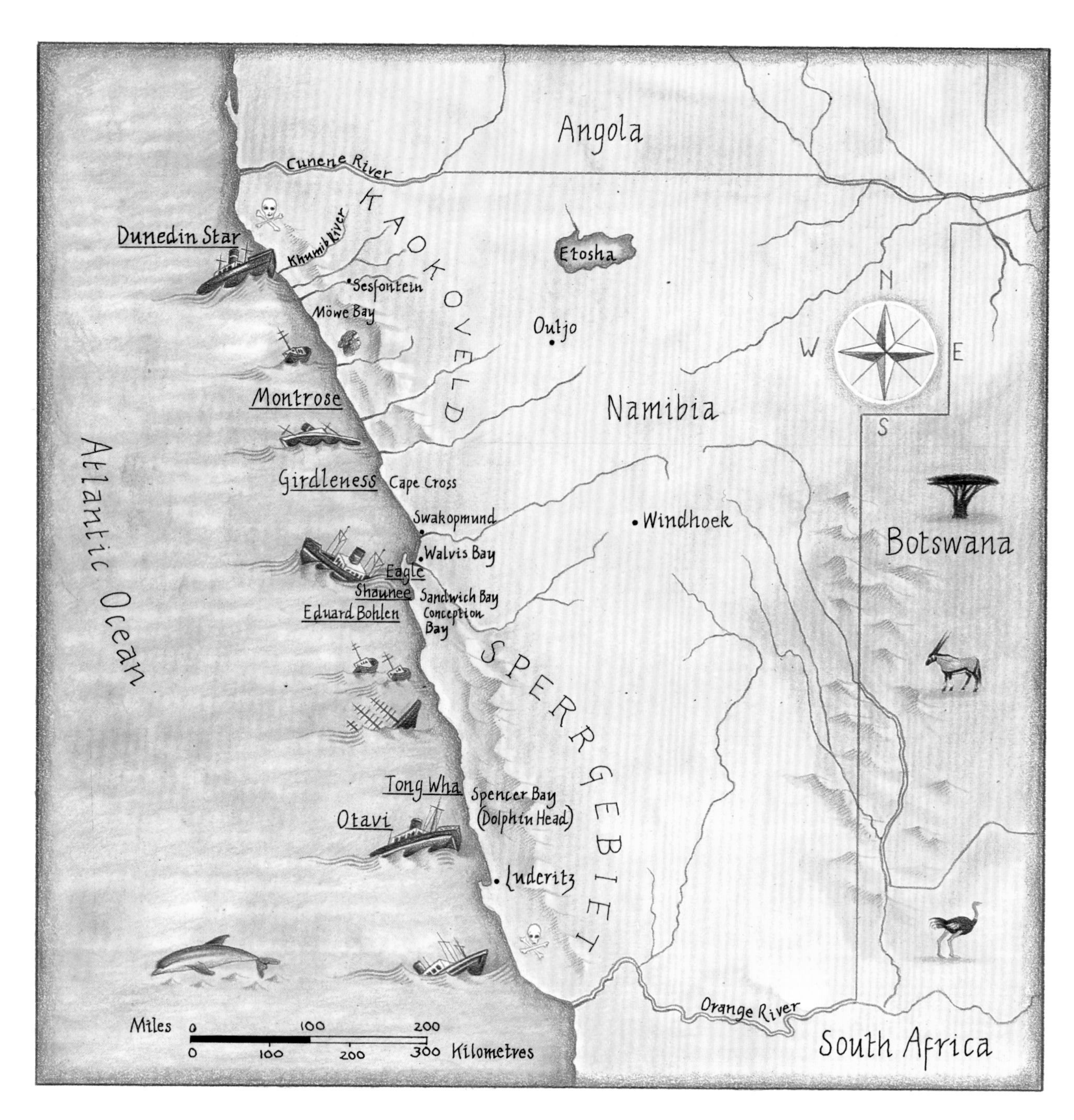

THE SKELETON COAST

Three more years were to pass before another opportunity arose to visit the area. It was April 1989 and I was gathering material for the book. On this occasion I was at last able to persuade the Nature Conservation and diamond authorities (CDM) to take me there by land. Each of them provided a four-wheel-drive vehicle. The CDM vehicle, equipped with a radio, was driven by Wynand Breytenbach from Luderitz and the Nature Conservation vehicle by Derek Clark. Derek was joined by his wife Jenny, who also works for Nature Conservation, and their dog. Together we set off and drove north in convoy from Luderitz on a journey which had once been described to me as impossible. To begin with we drove inland through the dunes, but later descended to the beach and raced for miles along the hard sand by the incoming surf.

We spent our first night at the old mining settlement of Saddle Hill, camping in the shell of an old house. Some of the houses were so buried in sand that only the roofs or chimneys were showing. Ours proved a welcome shelter from the fog and cold Atlantic winds. We made a roaring fire with driftwood and talked late into the night, so much so that the next morning I had difficulty persuading people to stir. It was after sunrise when we left and we drove through an awesome moonscape of crags and ridges, with coal-black seams running like roller-coasters through white, corrugated cliffs, interspersed with dunes of a similar size.

We wound our way through this wild and wonderful world until it opened out into a vast sandy plain, at the far side of which was Spencer Bay. Approaching the bay we came across a number of old jigs, screens and water barrels abandoned during the diamond days, which came to an end here in the 1920s. On the other side of a small ridge were three graves, lying side by side, made with black stones on the white sand. Perhaps they were diamond miners who died of thirst, or shipwrecked sailors who perished before help could reach them. There is a story of a four-master that was wrecked here in the mid-1800s and was later found by Hottentots, who apparently made several journeys to the bay to carry off the loot.

Leaving the vehicle near the foot of Dolphin Head, I went to look for my wreck while the rest of the party went off in search of a rare succulent (*Jensenobotrya lossowiana*) that grows there. I climbed over a two-hundred-foot ridge from where I could see the wreck of the *Otavi* in the bay below.

Having inspected the vessel from beach level I felt a boyish urge to climb aboard the wreck. The

FOLLOWING PAGES: *Dolphin Head towers above Spencer Bay and the wreck of the* Otavi *(1945). Nearby, on the beach, is a seal colony*

BELOW: *Wreck of the* Girdleness *near the mouth of the Ugab River*

ladders to the upper decks had all but rusted away, but I managed to reach the bridge and from here made progress along the upper deck, moving cautiously aft on the broken surface. I took some photographs and turned to go back when suddenly the rusted old deck gave way beneath me. Somehow I managed to stop myself plummeting through onto the jagged debris twenty feet below. I had cut my legs on the edge of the hole, but was otherwise all right. I realized that I would have to identify the beams and try not to tread between them, like stepping on rafters in an attic. I moved forward gingerly, but once again the deck collapsed and I clutched at an old guard rail where passengers had once stood, looking out to sea. It came away in my hand and I grabbed at something else, I don't know what, throwing myself away from the gaping hole. It was a miracle I did not go through. Everything was breaking up around me. As I straightened I noticed that my little finger was sticking out sideways at a bizarre ninety-degree angle, so I quickly twisted it back into line and felt an ominous click: a break or dislocation, I was not sure. Meanwhile I did not dare move for fear of falling through. But I knew that even if the others came looking for me they would never hear me

Wreck of the Otavi, *with a colony of Cape fur seals*

ABOVE: *The cliffs near Bogenfels, in the diamond area*

FOLLOWING PAGES: *The Bogenfels, a two-hundred-foot rock arch south of Pomona*

above the noise of the surf, and would certainly never find me if I fell below and injured myself. My only option was to take a chance and run for it, using speed to spread my weight. It took me a while to work up courage, but in the end I did run and the risk paid off. By the time I had climbed down to the beach I was shaking from shock and my finger was agony.

After this accident, I joined up with the rest of the party, who had found their succulent. Back at the vehicles, the conservator Derek Clark cut my signet ring from my swollen finger with some bolt-cutters to reduce the pain, and we set off north to look for another wreck I had spotted from the air in 1986. Our route took us over more mountains and dunes until we reached the area where I remembered the shipwreck to be. From here we walked down through the dunes to the shore, and coming round the point I spotted my wreck protruding from a sand dune about thirty feet above the level of the beach where an enormous storm must have hurled the bow section. Other bits of wreckage were still visible amongst the rocks below, the largest of which might have been a tank or boiler. I later discovered that the ship was Korean, and had sailed under the name of the *Tong Wha*. It came to grief nearly twenty years ago and the survivors were picked up by CDM's helicopter.

Over the centuries this coast has claimed thousands of ships and many more lives, which is why the name 'Skeleton Coast' was originally coined. Because of the changing nature of the

sea-bed, it is impossible to chart these waters with any degree of accuracy. Just as the desert dunes are always on the move, so the sand-bars on the sea-bed change their size, shape and position. This phenomenon, coupled with the fog and unpredictable currents, make it a mariner's nightmare. Nowadays ships are well equipped with sophisticated navigational tools and are thus not obliged to hug the coast, which gives them an advantage over their predecessors, who had to keep the land in sight partly for navigation reasons and partly because of their constant need for fresh water. The look-out in the crow's-nest had orders to report any signs of lakes or rivers inland. How many of these look-outs, I wonder, were deceived by mirages on salt-pans, and how many captains were tempted to investigate the reports. No doubt their bleached bones lie hidden beneath the sands.

Most of the wrecked early wooden ships rapidly disintegrated, battered by the heavy surf, yet some of them may await discovery under the dunes, shielded from the elements by the sand – ships that foundered in caves and inlets, thrown high and dry by the huge seas. In 1974, the conservator and former prospector Ernst Karlova caught sight of a piece of wood protruding from a dune on the northern Skeleton Coast. He recently described to me how 'something made me turn back and take a look at it. This was surprising when I think of the amount of driftwood I used to see along the coast.' To his amazement he found himself looking at the weathered remains of a great wooden face. He had discovered part of the oak figurehead from an old galleon, which experts have dated at around four hundred years old.

It was the Portuguese who pioneered this route down the west coast of Africa, followed later by the Dutch and British. The first voyage of discovery to sail as far south as the Namibian coast was

Figurehead from an old galleon, found in the dunes near Möwe Bay in 1974, which experts believe may be several hundred years old

made by Diego Cao in 1486, a few years before Columbus discovered the New World. The voyages of discovery were started in the early fifteenth century by Prince Henry the Navigator of Portugal. Official objectives at that time were more religious than commercial: the search for the fabled kingdom of Prester John, for example, that legendary Christian monarch who reigned somewhere in Eastern Africa, came high on the list. Diego Cao's objectives were, however, more commercially oriented. He was a knight in the court of King John II of Portugal, whose burning ambition was to find a trade route round the southern tip of Africa. In this way Portugal could gain access to the rich spice trade of the East. Cao's first two-year voyage took him as far as present-day Angola, where he planted 'padraos' (crosses) at the mouth of the Zaire (Congo) River, and at Cabo Do Lobo near present-day Namibe, formerly Mossamedes. It was on his second voyage that he reached Namibia and sailed as far as Cape Cross, about fifty miles south of the Ugab River. The place takes its name from the padrao he planted to commemorate his journey. At this point he was forced to turn back and, soon after his caravels had set sail, he died, his mission sadly unfulfilled. It was left to his successor, Bartholomew Diaz, to claim the honour of being the first European to sail round the Cape. When I visited Cape Cross a few years ago I found a granite replica of Cao's padrao which the Germans had erected in 1895. Nearby was a huge colony of seals.

In 1949 an old slate was found half buried in the sand, bearing a message dated 1860. 'I am proceeding to a river sixty miles north, and should anyone find this and follow me, God will help him.' History does not relate what became of this unfortunate castaway, but there seems little doubt that he perished, along with most of the other souls who were washed up on these lonely shores. There are several interesting records of early wrecks on this coast derived from a variety of sources. According to Gunter von Schumann, the Windhoek-based shipwreck enthusiast, one such record turned up when a certain Manuel Viegas was browsing through the Luanda archives, in Angola, in 1973. It stated that a British East Indiaman had been wrecked in the early 1700s near Angra Fria, about eighty miles south of the Cunene River. The vessel sprang a leak off the coast of West Africa and for a week the crew battled to prevent her from foundering. Then one morning they noticed brown seawater and floating driftwood, and because this obviously indicated a river mouth, they decided to run the ship ashore. It settled in the sand not far from the shore and there was panic as passengers and crew struggled to get to dry land. Many people were drowned but most of the crew reached safety. Exploring to the south of the wreck, they discovered a river in flood and constructed a makeshift camp from driftwood and flotsam. According to the report, many valuable items were recovered from the wreck, including spices, china, silk and jewellery.

At this stage there was a disagreement between the survivors over the best plan of action, and finally one group marched north along the beach while the rest stayed with the wreck. After some time, the walking group reached a river where they split up, one party continuing north along the beach and the other going inland up the river. After two days the inland group came into contact with some Africans who helped them get to Bahia Dos Tigres, fifty miles north of the Cunene in Angola. From here they were eventually picked up by a passing trading vessel from Sao Paulo de Luanda. The rest of the survivors were assumed to have perished.

The most celebrated wreck to have landed on the coast in recent times was that of the thirteen-thousand-ton *Dunedin Star*, a British liner that went aground during World War II between Angra Fria and the Cunene River. In 1942 the doomed ship was on a voyage between England and the Middle East with an important munitions cargo for the allied forces when disaster struck. She had been at sea for three weeks and her one hundred and six passengers and crew were looking forward to reaching Cape Town in only three days time. Late at night, however, on 29 November, she hit a submerged rock, thought to have been the Clan Alpine Shoal, which was marked on their map as being three to five miles offshore. Although the captain himself believed he was at least ten miles from the coast at the time of impact, the subsequent Court of Inquiry concluded that the ship might have been carried off course, and thus have hit the dreaded shoal. No other obstruction was marked on the chart and the only other object that she could have struck was a submarine. Whatever the hidden object was, the incident unleashed a dramatic chain of events involving rescue ships, aircraft and hundreds of courageous people. These events, and many others, were the subject of a book written by the maritime reporter John Marsh, entitled *Skeleton Coast*, first published in 1944. Incredibly only two people lost their lives in the epic rescue operation.

When Captain Lee, master of the *Dunedin Star*, realized the extent of the damage to his ship he headed straight for the mainland, anxious to beach her before she sank. It was a dangerous venture, charging full speed ahead through the night, having no idea what lay ahead. Had there been rocks offshore the ship could have ripped herself apart, but fortunately there were none, and eventually someone on the bridge caught sight of the white breakers ahead. Lee just had time to reduce speed and the ship went aground on a sandy beach. Skilfully, he eased her round so that she lay parallel to the surf and beach, facing southward. By the light of the stars they could just make out the desert stretching inland, with sand-dunes in the distance.

They had already sent out an SOS which had been received in Walvis Bay. Now they reported that they were aground and gave their position. The first rescuers to arrive on the scene were two ships that were in the general area, the *Temeraire*, a Norwegian ship, and the *Manchester Division*, a British freighter. In addition a minesweeper, the *Nerine*, and an ocean-going tug, the *Sir Charles Elliott*, were despatched to the scene from Walvis Bay. It took a good two days for them to reach the ship, during which time Captain Lee managed to get more than sixty passengers and crew to the beach, using one of the lifeboats which had a motor. He was worried that the *Dunedin Star* might break up, and the sooner the passengers were off the ship the better. After the lifeboat's second trip, however, a big wave threw it up on to the beach, disabling it. This was a major setback. Although the wreck was only two hundred yards from the beach, the surf was so heavy and the cross-currents so strong, that it was too dangerous for the passengers to cover the distance in a small boat or by swimming. From now on the beach party was on its own, with virtually no shelter and without food and water, and there was little that those on board could do about it. When the *Manchester Division* and *Temeraire* did arrive, it was the passengers on the wreck whom they were able to rescue and not the ones on the beach. Days later, the crew on the wreck managed to get a line to the beach party, along which some of the stronger passengers and crew pulled themselves back. Then a light surf-boat was also floated to the beach using a line, and a number of people returned to the wreck that way, until the surf-boat also capsized and was damaged. Attempts to float supplies to the beach were mainly unsuccessful because the rafts were caught by the cross-currents and carried miles to the north.

Soon after reaching the shore, some of the more adventurous survivors set off south along the beach in search of water and came across the remains of a wreck. There was a mast and a few old timbers and some crudely-constructed shelters nearby, half buried by sand. The timbers were old and rotten and the shelters were lined with frayed canvas. Digging around they found a large old bible and the remains of some shoes, and then they found bones. In all, they uncovered twelve skeletons, and what was particularly disturbing was that none of them had heads. Although they searched the area round the wreck thoroughly they never found the skulls.

OPPOSITE: *Wreck of the* Montrose *(1973) near Terrace Bay*

The rescue of the beach party now posed a major problem for the authorities. Those who were left were not strong enough to pull themselves to the wreck through the heavy surf, and they were the ones in the most urgent need of help. Conditions on the beach were extremely uncomfortable. At night they were soaked to the skin by the cold fogs, and were fried by day by the tropical sun. At other times they were blasted by gale-force winds that blew sand into their mouths, eyes and hair, added to which they were short of water and food. If they were to survive they would have to be rescued soon, yet there were no roads or towns within hundreds of miles of this remote coastline, and it was unlikely that an aircraft would be able to land in the vicinity. An aircraft could be used to drop supplies, though, and soon after the first messages had been received, the commander at Walvis Bay contacted Combined Headquarters in Cape Town asking for an aircraft to fly supplies to the survivors. A Ventura bomber was duly despatched, piloted by Captain Naude, which first landed at Walvis Bay to load up with food and water for the survivors.

With these arrangements under way a massive overland expedition was mounted from Windhoek, the convoy of trucks being expected to complete the six-hundred-mile journey through vast tracts of wilderness in three or four days. As things turned out it took the convoy nearly two back-breaking weeks to reach the wreck. After leaving Outjo, two hundred miles north of Windhoek, they suffered endless breakdowns, getting bogged down again and again in the heavy sand. Through an oversight, they had brought only one air pump for the tyres. They also had no radio, so for long periods no one had any idea where they were.

Meanwhile the sea rescue was proceeding relatively well, the remaining people on the *Dunedin Star* having been successfully transferred to the *Manchester Division* by volunteers from the *Temeraire*. The tug, the *Sir Charles Elliott*, had initially approached to within five feet of the wreck to see if anything could be done, but it was soon clear that the motor-boat from the *Temeraire* was doing everything possible to remove the passengers and crew to safety. The tug was also running low on coal and when she realized there was nothing more she could do, she weighed anchor and headed back for Walvis Bay. At about the same time the *Temeraire* also departed, having successfully completed the transfer operation to the *Manchester Division*. The *Nerine* was standing by to see what assistance she could offer.

The master of the tug, Captain Brewin, was exhausted after his long day manoeuvring the tug in difficult waters close to other shipping and on his return journey he handed over the watch at midnight and went to sleep in his cabin. A few hours later, in the early hours, he was woken by a terrible grinding, juddering noise and, rushing to the bridge, saw to his horror that they too were ashore. Somehow those treacherous currents had lured them off their course. Although he tried repeatedly to drag her off the rocks using his powerful engines, it was no good. The *Sir Charles Elliott* was doomed, and the Skeleton Coast had claimed another victim. Eventually Brewin got his men and himself to the beach by various means, but the lives of two of his deck-hands were lost in the process. One man was carried away by the current after the dinghy they were about to sail off in up-ended, pitching them into the surf. The other people on board miraculously survived, but another man later collapsed from exhaustion, and died, after battling in the surf trying to get in to the shore.

Brewin's first worry when his ship went aground was that he had no radio, so no one would know where he was. It was thus a welcome surprise when, about ten hours after the accident, someone caught sight of a plane flying north towards them up the coast. This was Captain Naude in his Ventura bomber, flying supplies to the *Dunedin Star* castaways.

Naude was astonished to see another beached ship, obviously not the *Dunedin Star*, and duly reported the wreck to Walvis Bay control. After circling the tug, he flew on to the big wreck and

CLOCKWISE FROM TOP LEFT: *The 13,000-ton* Dunedin Star, *aground on the Skeleton Coast, 1942; waves breaking over the decks of the stricken liner; rescue convoy struggling through the Kaokoveld; the rescue ship,* Sir Charles Elliott, *aground near Rocky Point* (*SA NAVAL ARCHIVES AND WINDHOEK ARCHIVES*)

successfully dropped his supplies in parachute containers. Some of these burst, especially the water containers, but a fair proportion landed intact. Having completed the drops, he looked around for a possible landing place. He had seen from the air that many of the survivors were in a poor way, and felt that if at all possible he should try to land and take some of the weaker women and children back to Walvis Bay. Selecting a flat piece of desert, he made a perfect landing, but when he taxied back to the starting point his wheels dug into the soft sand and the twelve-ton aircraft was well and truly stuck. Despite attempts by the castaways to dig the bomber out it dug in again every time. They were finally forced to give up, and by the time they had sent their radio messages explaining their situation, the aircraft's battery was all but dead.

A second Ventura bomber, flown by Major Robbs, was sent from Cape Town. It also took on supplies and fuel at Walvis Bay. Flying north it dropped some supplies for the *Sir Charles Elliott*'s castaways and continued to the *Dunedin Star*. When dropping his supplies, Robbs was less fortunate than Naude and most of his containers burst on impact. At Walvis Bay they had only been able to provide one twenty-gallon water container and even this split open because its parachute failed to open. The rest of the water had been loaded into inner tubes, every one of which burst when it hit the sand. Having circled its sand-bogged comrade, the second Ventura returned to Walvis Bay with the news that Naude would need assistance from overland. On his way south Robbs deviated to the east in the hope of spotting the overland convoy, but there was no sign of it. Several more supply flights followed, more effective than the previous drops, though much of the water was still lost. At the same time the minesweeper, the *Nerine*, which had returned to Walvis Bay with Captain Lee on board, was sent back to the wreck with a special surf-boat and crew, who were highly skilled at operating in these heavy conditions.

An attempt was now made to save the tug survivors, and a Ventura flown by Major Uys made a successful landing on a sandy ridge near Rocky Point, and took off again with eight of the more needy on board. Uys returned in his Ventura with a second plane, and together they were able to rescue the remaining members of the tug's crew, including Captain Brewin.

The other good news was that Major Robbs had at last spotted the overland convoy which had vanished into the Kaokoveld. He caught sight of tiny clouds of dust stirred up by the tracks as they made their way along the Khumib riverbed, down towards the sea. They were fifty miles from the *Dunedin Star* when he saw them, and less to the tug, yet those last fifty miles were to take the convoy another two whole days, thanks to the treacherous pans. To begin with the surface of these pans appeared hard and smooth, almost like tarmac, but as the trucks broke through the outer crust and sank to their axles, it turned into a quagmire. They could only move a few yards before having to dig each vehicle out again. Had one of the aircraft not dropped tarpaulins to them they could have been stuck there for weeks.

Three days after Major Robbs had first spotted the convoy in the Khumib valley, it finally reached the beach survivors. The surf-boat brought up by the *Nerine* had successfully taken twenty-six people off the beach before capsizing and being wrecked itself. There were, however, a number of people still awaiting rescue, particularly women and children, including the airmen whose bomber had got bogged in the sand, Captain Naude and his navigator. All the castaways, including some of their own rescuers, had now been saved. But the drama wasn't over.

As soon as Naude reached civilization, he was required to join an expedition that was returning by sea to the wreck site. The South African Air Force wanted to recover their Ventura bomber and

OPPOSITE: *The Langewand, or long mall, south of Sandwich Bay, a bleak landfall for shipwrecked sailors*

asked Naude to fly it out, using heavy wire netting as an improvised runway. Unfortunately the surf was so heavy that the recovery expedition failed, so another overland expedition was despatched, this time with a caterpillar tractor on board one of the trucks. The tractor was a godsend when the vehicles got bogged down, and they made better time than the rescue convoy. It took four days to service the Ventura and prepare her for action, and the tractor had no difficulty in pulling her out of the sand. With fresh batteries she started easily, and Naude managed a perfect take-off.

Heading south, he passed the wreck of the tug when his starboard engine suddenly seized. Unable to manoeuvre at such a low altitude, the bomber stalled and crashed into the sea. Miraculously neither he nor his crew members, Rudman and Bloemhof, were killed and they were able to reach the beach. Naude had injured an arm and a knee, and could only walk with difficulty. He was very much aware that the aircraft would not be missed for a long time since the Ventura's radio had been unserviceable and the convoy also had no radio contact with the authorities at Walvis Bay, who thus had no idea that he had taken off. The only hope of survival, he realized, was to try and intercept the returning recovery convoy, which would pass some thirty-two miles from where they had crashed. Walking all those miles in their bruised and shocked condition was no easy task. Rudman, who was the fittest, went on ahead to intercept the convoy and somehow they managed to get there before it passed. They were all rescued, and the saga of the *Dunedin Star* came to an end a lot more happily than could have been expected.

When I visited the site of the wreck a few months ago, the only relics left to mark it were a large tank, part of the ship's deck cargo, and the remains of the shelter which the castaways had erected from driftwood. Some of the upright poles are still standing. The wreck itself has been swallowed in its entirety by the sands, along with its valuable cargo of aircraft, trucks, guns, tanks and other military equipment, which was never salvaged.

One of the very few wrecks to have remained relatively intact, and the largest on the Namib coastline, is the *Eduard Bohlen*, which came to grief about eighty miles south of Walvis Bay. Owing to the changing nature of the shoreline, she now lies about half a mile inland, in the Sperrgebiet, as though she had sailed through the desert. When I visited Namibia in 1985 with a friend of mine, Angela Fisher (also a photographer), in order to collect material for an article on the Namib, I decided to visit the wreck. No one had been there for many years and access was difficult. I obtained permission from CDM to enter the Sperrgebiet on condition that I could show that I had a safe way of getting to the wreck. In Walvis Bay I was told that there were three alternatives. We could either go by land, or by sea or by air.

The problem with the first alternative was the sixty miles of huge dunes we would have to negotiate. This would mean organizing a specially-equipped convoy because one could not travel in one vehicle alone, and since CDM were not prepared to allow a large party to enter the diamond area this option appeared to be a non-starter. Down at the harbour I talked to a man with a fleet of fishing boats about the second alternative. He was keen to take us and seemed confident that he could land us near the wreck, but we would have to wait for calmer weather. The surf was too heavy at the moment and even if it calmed down sufficiently for him to drop us nearby, he could not guarantee when he would be able to pick us up again. It all sounded much too vague for my liking. The Skeleton Coast was not a place to be stranded.

I enquired about pilots for the third alternative and was told about a man called Martin Bertens who lived at Swakopmund. He had covered every inch of Namibia by air and if he could not take us there, no other pilot could. I found him at the local yacht club and, though sceptical at first, he soon warmed to the idea. For him it would, after all, be a rare opportunity to visit an area to which he was not normally allowed to fly. Browsing over the map he recalled how he had once landed at

Conception Bay to rescue some shipwrecked fishermen. At that time he had found a narrow strip of ground which had supported a narrow-gauge railway line during the diamond rush, leading from the bay to the nearby diamond mining settlements. The tracks themselves had long since rusted away, but from the air you could still see the marks left by the sleepers. If we were prepared to walk to the wreck from there, and return to the same place to be picked up, he could perhaps help us. He estimated the distance from the landing strip to the wreck at fifteen miles. At last we had found a 'safe' way of reaching the *Eduard Bohlen*.

Two days later we took off from Swakopmund airfield at sunrise, and headed south along the coast. Near Walvis Bay we overflew an island packed with seals, followed by a lagoon studded with thousands of flamingos, which rose in the air as we passed like confetti spiralling in the wind. Next came Sandwich Bay, with its long lagoon and hosts of pelicans, cormorants and countless other birds. From the air I spotted a jackal climbing the dunes, and saw him turn and stare as we flew by. We passed the wreck of the *Eagle* (see pp. 100 and 104) and, further south, flew low over the beach, with sand-dunes towering above us and blue-green breakers passing under our wheels. We saw seals and several huge whale bones and circled the remains of the *Shaunee*, a US supply ship, which went aground in 1976. Inland the dunes stretched away to the eastern horizon, wild and forbidding. I thought of Hans Kriess's story of the ox-wagons which came this way to the diamond fields.

Ribs and spars protruding from the sand – all that remains of the Eagle, *wrecked at Sandwich Bay in 1861*

Conception Bay came into view and then the wreck itself, clearly visible from this altitude. We located the old railway strip without much trouble and Martin made a perfect landing on a good, firm surface. Near where we stopped I inspected a pile of old rail tracks which fell to dust when touched. There was a beautiful clarity to the air and a purity to the scene which played tricks with perspective. The sand-dunes further east looked two or three minutes' walk from where we stood, but were probably a mile away or more. The sandy ground was studded with chips of quartz and agate, which sparkled like millions of eyes in the morning sunlight.

Martin had to return to Swakopmund for another appointment so we arranged to meet him back at the 'strip' the following afternoon. The aircraft lifted off, disappearing over the dunes to the north, and we were alone at Conception Bay in the Sperrgebiet.

From the air our route to the wreck had looked straightforward but on the ground we could not see it at all. Shouldering our packs we set out across a huge pan whose surface crust gave way beneath our weight. Once this pan had been part of the bay, but the coastline had changed and now the sea was out of sight a mile or more to the west. As the day grew hotter and the air began to dance it became more difficult to hold a course across the desert. My system of navigation was to take a 'fix' on a distant dune, yet as we approached, the dune would turn out to be a mirage. The desert was deceiving us and when I did find a dune I immediately climbed it before it could disappear. From the top I hoped to see the wreck, but was disappointed. All around were dunes and sand

The Eduard Bohlen *went aground near Conception Bay in 1909. On a voyage between Europe and Cape Town she stopped off to deliver mining equipment to the newly-opened diamond fields near Conception Bay. While manoeuvring in thick fog, she hit a sand-bar and stuck fast*

Postcard written from the Eduard Bohlen *by one of the passengers*

stretching away in every direction. Nowhere was there a sign of a wreck and I began to worry that we might have strayed off course. Looking down something strange caught my eye, not a ship's mast, but a pair of wheel tracks leading straight out from underneath my dune. They were clearly visible for fifty yards and then disappeared altogether. What puzzled me was the narrowness of the tracks. They were obviously very old and my dune had moved across them in the intervening years. Suddenly I realized that they were probably ox-wagon tracks that had been preserved for nearly seventy years.

From the next dune I climbed I saw the wreck, a small jagged silhouette on the southern horizon, continuously changing its shape in the haze. We were on course, and from now on it was easier having our objective in view. As we walked we saw several huge bones far inland, giving testimony to the slaughter of whales during the 1800s when this was still sea. I also saw what looked like spars protruding from the sand about half a mile away between us and the sea. Later I found that this might have been the remains of the *Cawdor Castle*, which foundered in 1926 with its cargo of 10,000 cases of Scotch whisky.

Gradually the wreck loomed into view until we stood at the base of the dune which had formed round her bows. This was an exciting moment. We had at last reached the *Eduard Bohlen*, a golden ghostship sailing into the desert. The sea was out of sight and earshot, a long way to the west. There was only silence and a piece of history locked in time. There were no human footprints to mar the purity of the wind-blown sand, only a line of jackal prints leading up the dune on to the bows. The ship was surprisingly big and while the bows were almost buried by sand, the stern stood proud with the rudder clearly visible. Built for the Woermann Line, today known as the Deutsche Afrika Linien (DAC), the *Bohlen* was launched in Hamburg, Germany in 1890. For nineteen years she steamed up and down the West African Coast between Europe and the Cape, carrying her passengers and cargo. It was the summer of 1909, the year my father was born, and the *Bohlen* was

sailing south, having recently left Europe laden with luxury goods and equipment. Most of this cargo was destined for the newly-opened South West African diamond fields and the *nouveau-riche* society that had blossomed in the desert. After stopping at the diamond ports her skipper, Captain Parrow, would take her on to Cape Town to load up for the return journey. In the *Bohlen*'s cargo was a consignment of diamond equipment to be delivered to the new mining settlements near Conception Bay. It was early morning and Captain Parrow was manoeuvring in the fog towards a point where he could drop his cargo, when his ship hit a sand-bar ten miles south of the bay and stuck solid. Try as he might, Parrow could not free his ship and, according to reports, even jettisoned some of his cargo in an effort to refloat her. He must have been more than aware that this was the end of the road, not only for his ship but most likely for him too, as a skipper. This was the second ship that had been lost under his command on the Skeleton Coast. In 1903 he had been in command of the coaster *Gertrude Woermann I* when she was lost at Port Nolloth, near the Orange River mouth, and it was after this that he was given command of the *Eduard Bohlen*.

When the *Bohlen* went aground, she bestowed a quantity of unexpected gifts on the recently-arrived fortune seekers in the area. Suddenly there was a plethora of free tinned ham, cognac and Schiedam gin, with other mouth-watering luxuries to add variety to their tables. In the meantime the wreck itself was purchased by one of the passengers, Hermann Offen, who, believe it or not, had plans to drag the ship to open water using spans of oxen. Initially it was used to house migrant labourers from the mining company, and after the accident there was merry-making and high living on board for a while, with the manager living in the Captain's quarters. 'What should we drink tonight, Sir?' the steward might have asked. 'A little Moselle 1902 or perhaps a Château Latour 1887.'

OPPOSITE: *'We camped near the wreck and the following morning I went on board to explore, carefully testing the surfaces with my feet. The cabins smelt of dead sea-birds. So I climbed the companionway to the upper deck and looked out over the desert'*

BELOW: *One of many castaways who perished on this coast*

Launched in Hamburg in 1890, the Eduard Bohlen *was one of the first steamships built by the Woermann Line, yet it was some years before sails were finally dispensed with. In this painting,* Under Sail and Steam, *artist Keith Alexander shows the* Eduard Bohlen *as she might have appeared prior to 1909 (COLLECTION: DEUTSCHE AFRIKA LINIEN, HAMBURG, formerly the Woermann Line)*

During these years ships out to sea often saw the lights on board, because people made fires in the cabins, and thought they had seen a ghostship. That was all a long time ago, of course, before World War I. Nevertheless, I found several old champagne bottles weathered and sculpted by seventy-five years of wind-blown sand. Nearby were hummocks of sand, concealing piles of wood, presumably from old cabin fittings, along with ropes, chairs and bits of machinery that fell to pieces when touched. Heaps of fabric, old medicine bottles and plates all lay buried in the sand.

As we were inspecting these remains the sun disappeared behind a wall of fog advancing into the desert. An icy wind blew from the Atlantic and we hastily set about erecting our tent. This was easier said than done because ordinary pegs were instantly jerked out by the wind. The solution, I discovered, was to fashion stakes from old wooden planks and these held up well. Two large timbers served as a barrier preventing the wind from undermining the tent. We used a whole box of matches to get a fire going nearby, but this gave precious little warmth. Retreating into the tent we lit the gas cooker and huddled round it.

We woke to a cold damp morning with the wreck looming eerily from the fog. After a mug of hot tea, I began to explore and climbed on board, carefully testing the surfaces with my feet. Most of the bow section was filled with sand, as I suspected, and the interior of the stern had collapsed within its outer shell. Only the upper part of the middle section was relatively intact and accessible.

Here I was able to peer into cabins and tried to imagine life on board prior to September 1909. The gloomy interiors smelt of dead sea-birds so I climbed the companion-way to the upper deck. Some of the handrails were still in place and the wooden deck planks on the starboard side of the bows were in excellent condition, almost ready for a game of 'deck-quoits'.

I stood there, absorbing the stillness, pondering the incongruity of this desert ship. Closing my eyes I pictured the scene when she left Hamburg on her final voyage to Africa. Her passengers waved good-bye from here, and on previous trips would have stood entranced by their first view of Table Mountain when the ship finally sailed into Table Bay. It was possible that some of these passengers were still alive, though unlikely. It would be strange to bring them back and show them this scene today. In this little patch of desert, human history had come and gone almost unnoticed by the wider world, leaving its fragile stamp on the sands. Here was a symbol of man's brief presence in a timeless wilderness.

FOLLOWING PAGES: *Shipwreck cast up on a lonely stretch of the Skeleton Coast*

BELOW: *'I stood there . . . pondering the incongruity of this desert ship. . . . If any passengers were still alive . . . it would be strange to bring them back and show them the scene today'*

BIBLIOGRAPHY

Andersson, Carl J., *Exploration and Discoveries in South Western Africa*, Cape Town, 1967

Bannister, Anthony and Johnson, Peter, *Namibia: Africa's Harsh Paradise*, Struik, Cape Town, 1978; Country Life Books, London, 1979

Bradford, Ernle, *Southward the Caravels. The Story of Henry the Navigator*, Hutchinson, London, 1961

Brittan, Michael, *Discover Namibia*, Struik, Cape Town, 1979

Cornell, F. C., *The Glamour of Prospecting*, Fisher Unwin, London, 1920; new facsim. ed. David Philip, London, 1986

Coulson, David, 'A Race Against Time', *Departures* (American Express magazine), London, September 1988

Coulson, David, 'The Wild Horses of the Namib', *Optima* (Journal of the Anglo-American and De Beers group of companies), London, March 1987

Coulson, David and Clarke, James, *Mountain Odyssey in Southern Africa*, Macmillan (SA), Johannesburg, 1983

Cubitt, Gerald and Richter, Johann, *South West*, Struik, Cape Town, 1976; Cassell, London, 1978

Dorst, J. and Dandelot, P., *A Field Guide to the Larger Mammals of Africa* (2nd ed.), Collins, London, 1980

Green, Lawrence G., *Lords of the Last Frontier*, Howard B. Timmins, Cape Town, 1952; Stanley Paul, London, 1972

Harper, Sally, 'The Schutztruppe', *Rössing* (Journal of RTZ Uranium, Namibia), Windhoek, September 1982

Jackman, Brian and Coulson, David, 'Hell is for Horses', *Sunday Times Magazine*, London, October 1987

Jacobson, Leon and Noli, Dieter, 'An eye witness account of coastal settlement and subsistence along the northern Namibian coast', *The South African Archaeological Bulletin*, 1987

Jenkins, Geoffrey, *A Twist of Sand*, Fontana, London, 1961; originally Collins, London, 1959

Katz, Richard, *Boiling Energy: Community Healing Among the Kalaharisan*, Harvard University Press, Cambridge, Mass. and London, 1982

Le Roux, A. and Schelpe, E., *Namaqualand and Clanwilliam*, Botanical Society of South Africa, Cape Town, 1981

Lee, Richard, *The ! Kung San. Men, Women and Children in a Foraging Society*, Cambridge University Press, 1979

Leutwein, von Theodor, *Elf Jahre Gouverneur in Deutsch-Südwest-Afrika*, E. Mitler, Berlin, 1908

Levinson, Olga, *Diamonds in the Desert*, Tafelberg, Cape Town, 1983

Loutit, Blythe, 'The Damaraland Rhino', *African Wildlife*, Cape Town, vol. 42, no. 2, March/April 1988

Loutit, Blythe, 'The Skeleton Coast', *African Wildlife*, Cape Town, vol. 42, no. 2, March/April 1988

Loutit, Blythe and Lindeque, Malan, 'A great step for the Desert Giants', *Quagga* (Journal of the Endangered Wildlife Trust of Southern Africa), Johannesburg, Autumn 1987

Malan, J. S., *Peoples of South West Africa/Namibia*, Haum, Pretoria, 1980

Marsh, John, *Skeleton Coast*, Hodder & Stoughton, London and Cape Town, 1944

Martin, Henno, *The Sheltering Desert* (English ed.), William Kimber, London, 1957

Merensky, H., 'How I found the richest diamond fields in the world', *The Mining and Industrial Magazine* (SA), Johannesburg, May 1927

Mossolow, N., 'Duwisib Castle', *Rössing*, Windhoek, April 1981

Newman, Kenneth, *Newman's Birds of Southern Africa*, Macmillan (SA), Johannesburg, 1984

Noli, Dieter and Avery, Graham, 'Stone Circles in the Cape Fria area, Northern Namibian Coast', *The South African Archaeological Bulletin*, Cape Town, 1987

Owen-Smith, Garth, 'There is Another Way', *Quagga*, Johannesburg, Autumn 1987

Palgrave, Keith Coates, *Trees of Southern Africa*, Struik, Cape Town, 1977

Phillips, John A. S., 'Bismarck and Sudwestafrika', *Rössing*, Windhoek, October 1985

Reardon, Mitch, *Besieged Desert*, Collins, London, 1986

Roberts, Austin, *Roberts' Birds of Southern Africa*, John Voelcker Book Fund, Cape Town, 1985

Schoeman, Amy, *Skeleton Coast*, Macmillan (SA), Johannesburg, 1984

Schoeman, Amy, 'Xerophytic Plants of Namibia', *Rössing*, Windhoek, April 1984

Seely, Mary, *The Namib*, Shell Oil Ltd, Windhoek, 1987

Smithers, Reay H. N., *The Mammals of the Southern African Subregion*, University of Pretoria, 1983

van der Merwe, Professor F., *Notes on a Herd of Wild Horses*, Pretoria, 1986

van der Post, Laurens, *A Far Off Place*, Penguin Books, London, 1976

van der Post, Laurens, *The Heart of the Hunter*, Chatto & Windus, London, 1969

Vedder, Heinrich, *The Peoples of South West Africa*, Windhoek, 1937

Vedder, Heinrich, *South West Africa in Early Times*, Oxford University Press, 1988

Viljoen, Slang, 'The Desert-Dwelling Elephant', *African Wildlife*, Cape Town, vol. 42, no. 2, March/April 1988

von Schumann, Gunter, 'Lost Treasures of the Skeleton Coast', *Rössing*, Windhoek, September 1982

Ward, J., Seely, M. and Lancaster, N., 'On the Antiquity of the Namib', *South African Journal of Science*, vol. 79 (175/83), Pretoria, 1978

Wellington, J. H., *South West Africa and its Human Issues*, Clarendon Press, Oxford, 1967

Williams, Tony, 'Walvis Bay and Other Coastal Gems', *African Wildlife*, Cape Town, vol. 42, no. 2, March/April 1988

Witbooi, Hendrik, *His Daybook (1885–1894)*, Windhoek Archives

Woodhouse, H. C., *Archaeology in Southern Africa*, Purnell, London and Cape Town, 1971

INDEX

Page numbers in *italic* refer to the illustrations